D1633109

Real

Listening & Speaking 2
with answers

Sally Logan and Craig Thaine

HARROW COLLEGE
EFL CENTRE

CAMBRIDGE UNIVERSITY PRESS

CAMBRIDGE UNIVERSITY PRESS
Cambridge, New York, Melbourne, Madrid, Cape Town, Singapore, São Paulo, Delhi

Cambridge University Press
The Edinburgh Building, Cambridge CB2 8RU, UK

www.cambridge.org
Information on this title: www.cambridge.org/9780521702003

First published 2008

Printed in the United Kingdom at the University Press, Cambridge

A catalogue record for this publication is available from the British Library

ISBN-13 978-0-521-70200-3

Contents

Map of the book

Unit number	Title	Topic	How to ...
Social and Travel			
1	How do you know Mark?	Socializing	• make and answer invitations • start conversations • take part in 'small talk' conversations
2	I'm phoning about the house	Living away from home	• check you have understood information correctly • ask polite questions to find out information • describe a problem and suggest a solution
3	How do I buy a ticket?	Transport	• understand information about public transport • ask for travel information • check your understanding of information
4	Shall we go out for dinner?	Eating out	• make suggestions • understand descriptions of food and meals • talk about what you ate in a restaurant
5	You should go to the police	Emergencies	• speak without repeating unnecessary words • understand information about personal details and events • give general and detailed descriptions
6	Have you got a headache?	Health	• understand medicine instructions • give instructions and advice • explain what something is
7	How about a hostel?	Holiday accommodation	• ask about different kinds of accommodation • understand information about accommodation • describe rooms and objects
8	What can I do here?	Sightseeing	• show you understand what someone is saying and that you are interested • talk about what you want and would like to do • book an activity at a Tourist Information Centre

Acknowledgements

The authors would like to thank the team at Cambridge University Press for their ongoing encouragement, support and expertise, in particular Noírín Burke, Caroline Thiriau, Hazel Meek, Barbara Thomas and Linda Matthews, as well as the team at Kamae Design. They would also like to thank colleagues, students and friends who contributed to the dialogues in this book.

Sally Logan would like to thank Taner Erdi for his encouragement and support, and Emre Logan-Erdi for making things manageable.

Craig Thaine would like to thank Steven Shuttleworth for ongoing encouragement, patience and support.

Special thanks too, to Ann and Brian Giles for the photograph on page 14.

The authors and publishers are grateful for the following reviewers for their valuable insights and suggestions:

Kathryn Alevizos, UK
Steven Banfield, UAE
Nigel Daly, Taiwan
Rui da Silva, UK
Stephanie Dimond-Bayir, UK
Rosie Ganne, UK
Barbara Gardner, UK
Hebe Gomez, Spain
Professor Peter Gray, Japan
Duncan Hindmarch, UK
Dr Zbigniew Mozejko, Poland
Paul Seligson, UK
Raymond Sheehan, UAE

The authors and publishers acknowledge the following sources of copyright material and are grateful for the permissions granted. While every effort has been made, it has not always been possible to identify the sources of all the material used, or to trace all copyright holders. If any omissions are brought to our notice, we will be happy to include the appropriate acknowledgements on reprinting.

P. 20: the Rainbow Card and the No-My-Car-Day Pass with kind permission of the Osaka Transportation Bureau.

The publishers are grateful to the following for permission to reproduce copyright photographs and material:

Key: l = left, c = centre, r = right, t = top, b = bottom

Alamy/©Marc Romanelli for p. 16, /©Jon Bower for p. 18, /©Stockfolio for p31, /©Danita Delimont for p. 36, /©Gregory Bajor for p. 42, /©Iconotec for p43 (b), / ©J G Photography for p. 54 (c), /©Image 100 for p. 64; Corbis Images/©Zefa/Grace for p. 10, /©Gunter Marx Photography for p. 34, /©Hoberman Collection for p. 43 (c), /©Benjamin Lowry for p. 54 (t); Getty Images/©Superstudio for p. 52, /©Iconica for p. 68; New Zealand Skydive for p. 40; Punchstock/©Inspirestock for p. 22; Rex Features for pp. 39 and 54 (b); Travel Library/©Chris Hermes for p. 43 (t).

Illustrations

Kathy Baxendale pp. 29, 61; Paco Cavero pp. 46, 47; Mark Duffin pp. 14, 30b, 32t, 37, 52, 60; Katie Mac pp. 12, 32b, 38, 63, 70, 73; Laura Martinez pp. 24, 28, 56, 58, 72; Julian Mosedale pp. 16, 44; Rory Walker pp. 30, 75; Ian West pp. 23, 26, 48, 65.

Text design and page make-up: Kamae Design, Oxford
Cover design: Kamae Design, Oxford
Cover photo: © Getty Images
Picture research: Hilary Luckcock

Introduction

To the student

Who is *Real Listening & Speaking 2* for?

You can use this book if you are a student at pre-intermediate level and you want to improve your English listening and speaking. You can use the book alone without a teacher or you can use it in a classroom with a teacher.

How will *Real Listening & Speaking 2* help me with my listening and speaking?

Real Listening & Speaking 2 contains practical tasks to help you in everyday situations, e.g. at a party, in a restaurant or travelling away from home. It also gives practice of listening and speaking in a range of work and study situations. It is designed to help you with listening and speaking you will need to do when communicating in English at home or when visiting another country.

The exercises in each unit help you to develop useful listening skills such as listening for opinions, listening for details, and listening for the main idea. There are also lots of practical speaking strategies and tasks to help you improve your ability to communicate, and pronunciation activities too.

How is *Real Listening & Speaking 2* organized?

The book has 16 units and is divided into two sections:
- Units 1–10 – social and travel situations
- Units 11–16 – work and study situations

Every unit has:
- *Get ready to listen and speak:* introduces you to the topic of the unit
- *Learning tip:* helps you improve your learning
- *Class bonus:* is an exercise you can do with other students or friends
- *Speaking strategy:* gives you useful language and strategies for communicating
- *Speak up!:* gives you practice of speaking in real situations
- *Extra practice:* gives an extra exercise for more practice
- *Can-do checklist:* helps you think about what you learnt in the unit

Most units also have:
- *Focus on*: helps you study useful grammar or vocabulary
- *Did you know?*: gives you extra information about vocabulary, different cultures or the topic of the unit
- *Sound smart:* helps you with pronunciation

After each main section there is a review unit. The reviews help you practise the skills you learn in each section.

At the back of the book you can find:
- *Appendices:* contain lists of *Useful language*, Listening and Speaking learning tips, and worksheets for listening to the news, watching movies and planning your learning.
- *Audioscript:* includes everything that you can hear on the audio CDs and gives information about the nationalities of the speakers
- *Answer key:* gives correct answers and possible answers for exercises that have more than one answer

How can I use *Real Listening & Speaking 2*?

The book is in two sections; *Social and Travel*, and *Work and Study*. The units at the end of the book are more difficult than the units at the beginning of the book. However, you do not need to do the units in order. It is better to choose the units that are most interesting for you and to do them in the order you prefer.

There are many different ways you can use this book. We suggest you work in this way:
- Look in the *Contents* list and find a unit that interests you.
- Go to *Appendix 1* and look at the *Useful language* for the unit you want to do. You can use a dictionary to help you understand the words and expressions.
- Do the *Get ready to listen and speak* section at the start of the unit. This will introduce you to the topic of the unit.
- Do the other exercises in the unit. At the end of each exercise check your answers in the *Answer key*.
- If your answers are wrong, study the section again to see where you made mistakes.
- Try to do the listening exercises without looking at the audioscript. You can read the audioscript after you finish the exercises.
- If you want to do more work on this topic, do the *Extra practice* activity.
- At the end of the unit, think about what you learnt and complete the *Can-do checklist.*
- Go to *Appendix 1* and look at the *Useful language* for the unit again.

Introduction
To the teacher

What is *Cambridge English Skills*?

Real Listening & Speaking 2 is one of 12 books in the *Cambridge English Skills* series. The series also contains *Real Reading* and *Real Writing* books and offers skills training to students from elementary to advanced level. All the books are available in with-answers and without-answers editions.

Level	Book	Author
Elementary CEF: A2 Cambridge ESOL: KET NQF Skills for life: Entry 2	Real Reading 1 with answers	Liz Driscoll
	Real Reading 1 without answers	Liz Driscoll
	Real Writing 1 with answers and audio CD	Graham Palmer
	Real Writing 1 without answers	Graham Palmer
	Real Listening & Speaking 1 with answers and audio CDs (2)	Miles Craven
	Real Listening & Speaking 1 without answers	Miles Craven
Pre-intermediate CEF: B1 Cambridge ESOL: PET NQF Skills for life: Entry 3	Real Reading 2 with answers	Liz Driscoll
	Real Reading 2 without answers	Liz Driscoll
	Real Writing 2 with answers and audio CD	Graham Palmer
	Real Writing 2 without answers	Graham Palmer
	Real Listening & Speaking 2 with answers and audio CDs (2)	Sally Logan & Craig Thaine
	Real Listening & Speaking 2 without answers	Sally Logan & Craig Thaine
Intermediate to upper-intermediate CEF: B2 Cambridge ESOL: FCE NQF Skills for life: Level 1	Real Reading 3 with answers	Liz Driscoll
	Real Reading 3 without answers	Liz Driscoll
	Real Writing 3 with answers and audio CD	Roger Gower
	Real Writing 3 without answers	Roger Gower
	Real Listening & Speaking 3 with answers and audio CDs (2)	Miles Craven
	Real Listening & Speaking 3 without answers	Miles Craven
Advanced CEF: C1 Cambridge ESOL: CAE NQF Skills for life: Level 2	Real Reading 4 with answers	Liz Driscoll
	Real Reading 4 without answers	Liz Driscoll
	Real Writing 4 with answers and audio CD	Simon Haines
	Real Writing 4 without answers	Simon Haines
	Real Listening & Speaking 4 with answers and audio CDs (2)	Miles Craven
	Real Listening & Speaking 4 without answers	Miles Craven

Where are the teacher's notes?

The series is accompanied by a dedicated website containing detailed teaching notes and extension ideas for every unit of every book. Please visit www.cambridge.org/englishskills to access the *Cambridge English Skills* teacher's notes.

What are the main aims of *Real Listening & Speaking 2*?

- To encourage autonomous learning by focusing on learner training
- To help students develop listening and speaking skills in accordance with the ALTE (Association of Language Testers in Europe) Can-do statements. These statements describe what language users can typically do at different levels and in different contexts. Visit www.alte.org for further information.

What are the key features of *Real Listening & Speaking 2*?

- It is aimed at pre-intermediate learners of English at level B1 of the Council of Europe's CEFR (Common European Framework of Reference for Languages)
- It contains 16 four-page units, divided into two sections: Social and Travel, and Work and Study.
- *Real Listening and Speaking 2* units contain:
  - *Get ready to listen and speak* warm-up tasks to get students thinking about the topic
  - *Learning tip* boxes which give students advice on how to improve their listening and speaking and their learning
  - *Focus on* activities which provide contextualized practice in particular language or vocabulary areas
  - *Sound smart* activities which focus on pronunciation
  - *Class bonus* communication activities for pairwork and group work so you can adapt the material to suit your classes
  - *Did you know?* boxes which provide notes on cultural or linguistic differences between English-speaking countries, or factual information on the topic of the unit
  - *Can-do checklists* at the end of every unit to encourage students to think about what they have learnt
- There are two review units to practise skills that have been introduced in the units.
- It covers a wide range of highly practical activities that give students the skills they need to communicate effectively in everyday situations.
- It has an international feel and contains a range of native and non-native English accents.
- It can be used as self-study material, in class, or as supplementary homework material.

What is the best way to use *Real Listening & Speaking 2* in the classroom?

The book is designed so that there is no set way to work through the units. The units may be used in any order, although the more difficult units naturally appear near the end of the book, in the *Work and Study* section.

You can consult the unit-by-unit teacher's notes at www.cambridge.org/englishskills for detailed teaching ideas. However, as a general guide, different parts of the book can be approached in the following ways:

- *Useful language:* Use the *Useful language* lists in the *Appendices* to preteach or revise the vocabulary from the unit you are working on.
- *Get ready to listen and speak:* It is a good idea to use this section as an introduction to the topic. Students can work on these exercises in pairs or groups. Many of these exercises require students to answer questions about their personal experience. These questions can be used as prompts for discussion. Some exercises contain a problem-solving element that students can work on together. Other exercises aim to clarify key vocabulary in the unit. You can present these vocabulary items directly to students.
- *Learning tips:* Focus on these and draw attention to them in an open class situation. An alternative approach is for you to create a series of discussion questions associated with the *Learning tip*. Students can discuss their ideas in pairs or small groups followed by open class feedback. The *Learning tip* acts as a reflective learning tool to help promote learner autonomy.
- *Class bonuses:* The material in these activities aims to provide freer practice. You can set these up carefully, then take the role of observer during the activity so that students carry out the task freely. You can make yourself available to help students or analyze the language they produce during the activity.
- *Extra practice:* These can be set as homework or out-of-class projects for your students. Students can do some tasks in pairs during class time.
- *Can-do checklists:* Refer to these at the beginning of a lesson to explain to students what the lesson will cover, and again at the end so that students can evaluate their learning for themselves.
- *Appendices:* You may find it useful to refer your students to these.
- *Audioscript:* Occasionally non-native speaker spoken errors are included in the audio material. They are labelled *Did you notice?* in the audioscript and can be used in the classroom to focus on common errors.

Unit 1
How do you know Mark?

Get ready to	**listen and speak**

- Look at the activities below and tick ✓ the ones you like doing.

  going to the cinema ☐ playing sport ☐ listening to music ☐ cooking ☐
  going to parties ☐ gardening ☐ going online ☐ visiting relatives ☐
  meeting friends ☐ going shopping ☐ drawing and painting ☐ playing musical instruments ☐
  watching sport ☐ going to restaurants ☐ playing computer games ☐ reading books and magazines ☐

- What do you and your friends usually do at the weekend?

  ----

go to Useful language p. 78

A Listening – Phoning a friend

1 🔲⓵② **Mark telephones his friend Brian on Sunday night. Listen to their conversation. What is the main reason for the phone call? Tick ✓ a, b or c.**

a to find out what Brian did at the weekend ☐
b to find out what Brian is doing next weekend ☐
c to invite Brian to a birthday party ☐

Learning tip

Try and understand the general meaning of a text before you listen for the details. Don't worry if you can't understand everything. Think about what you want to know and only listen for that information.

Did you know ...?

In the UK people say *go to the cinema*, but in the US they say *go to the movies*.

2 🔲⓵② **Brian tells you about Mark's party. He has got some of the information wrong. Read what Brian says, then listen again and correct his mistakes. The first mistake is corrected for you.**

> Mark called last night. It's his birthday ~~this~~ *next* week
>
> and he's having a party on Friday to celebrate.
>
> It starts at eight o'clock. He wants me to take
>
> some food. I'm looking forward to it.

3 🔲⓵③ **Listen to Brian telling you about Mark's party. He now has the correct information. Check your answers.**

B Speaking – Phoning a friend

Speaking strategy
Making and answering invitations

1 Look at the *audioscript* on page 88. Is the party the first thing Mark talks about?

YES / NO

2 Mark and Brian use the expressions below. Put them in the order they say them.

...... a Do you want me to bring anything?

...... b What day?

..1... c Actually the reason I'm ringing is because it's my birthday next week.

...... d What time?

...... e I was wondering if you wanted to come.

...... f That sounds good.

3 Which expression explains why Mark is phoning? ....

4 Which expression is an invitation? Which expression is a reply to an invitation? Write them below.

Invitation	Reply to invitation
I was wondering if you wanted to come	....
....	....
....	....
....	....
....	....

5 Now look at these expressions and put them in the table above.

Do you want to come?

Would you like to come?

That'd be nice.

I'd love to.

6 Look at the invitations in the table above. They are all polite but some are more polite. Put them in order of politeness: 1 = most polite, 3 = less polite.

7 Not everyone accepted Mark's invitation. Look at what they said and <u>underline</u> their reasons for not going to the party.

That sounds good but I'm afraid I'm going away at the weekend.

I'd really like to but I work on Saturday evenings.

When you say *no* to an invitation, it is important to explain why you can't go. It is also polite to say something positive first, e.g. *That sounds good but …* or *I'd really like to but …*

Sound smart
Missing sounds

1 🔊 **4** Listen to this question.
What day?
What sound is missing? Tick ✓ one of the sounds below.

/w/ ☐   /t/ ☐   /d/ ☐

2 Why is the missing sound not pronounced? Tick ✓ a, b or c.

a This is a natural way of linking words in sentences when speaking English. ☐

b Brian can't pronounce the words correctly. ☐

c Brian is lazy. ☐

3 🔊 **4** Listen to the question again and practise saying it. What day?

4 🔊 **5** Listen to these sentences and then practise saying them. Remember the <u>underlined</u> /t/ sounds at the end of the words are not pronounced.

a Do you wan<u>t</u> me to bring anything?

b Wha<u>t</u> time?

c Tha<u>t</u> sounds good.

Focus on ...
beginning and ending phone conversations

Which two of the expressions below (a–e) do Brian and Mark use at the beginning of the conversation? Write *Beginning* next to them.

Which three expressions do they use at the end of the conversation? Write *End* next to them.

a Hello, Brian speaking. ....

b See you on Saturday. ....

c Hi Brian. It's Mark here. ....

d See you then. ....

e Bye for now. ....

Note: You can also say *This is Mark* instead of *It's Mark here.*

Speak up!

8 🔘6 Mark telephones you about his party. Read what he says and think about what you will say. Talk to Mark and find out about the party. Speak after the telephone rings.

You: Hello, (say your name) speaking.
Mark: Hi. It's Mark here.
You: ---
Mark: I'm fine. How are you?
You: ---
Mark: Have you had a good weekend?
You: ---
Mark: Not too bad. Actually the reason I'm ringing is because it's my birthday next week and I'm going to have a party. I was wondering if you wanted to come.
You: ---
Mark: Saturday night.
You: ---
Mark: About 7.30.
You: ---
Mark: No. I'll have food and everything.
You: ---
Mark: See you on Saturday. Bye.
You: ---

9 🔘7 Cover the conversation in Exercise 8. You are a friend of Brian's and you phone him to invite him to your birthday party. First read what Brian says and think about what you will say. Speak after Brian.

Brian: Hello, Brian speaking.
You: Hi Brian. It's (say your name) here.
Brian: Hi. How are you?
You: ---
Brian: Fine.
You: ---
Brian: Yes I have. I went to the cinema with some friends yesterday and I haven't done much today. What about you?
You: ---
Brian: That sounds good. What day?
You: ---
Brian: OK. What time?
You: ---
Brian: Do you want me to bring anything?
You: ---
Brian: OK. That sounds great. See you then.
You: ---
Brian: Bye.

Learning tip

Don't worry if you don't say the exact same words as the conversation. Try and say something that has a similar meaning. The more you try, the easier it will get.

C Listening – At a party

1 🔘8 Mark introduces Brian to some friends at the party. Listen to the conversation.

How many people are talking?
Tick ✓ a, b or c.
a two ☐
b three ☐
c four ☐

2 🔘8 Listen to the conversation again. Tick ✓ a, b or c.

1 Why does Mark leave the conversation?
  a to talk to other people ☐
  b to get some food ☐
  c to get something to drink ☐

2 Mark and Reshma are
  a friends from football. ☐
  b colleagues. ☐
  c neighbours. ☐

3 How long has Reshma known Mark?
  a two months ☐
  b one year ☐
  c two years ☐

D Speaking – At a party

Speaking strategy
Starting conversations

Look at how Brian and Mark start conversations.

Brian and I play football together.

How do you know Mark?

They focus on finding something in common:
– Brian and Mark both play football.
– Brian and Reshma both know Mark.

When you start a conversation with someone you do not know well, it is a good idea to find something you have in common.

Here are some ideas that are often used to make 'small talk' (informal conversation about everyday things):
– jobs
– where you are (e.g. the room, the view, the food and drink, the people)
– weather
– people's interests

1 Listen to other people at the party. Which of the topics above do they talk about?

Conversation A ⊙ 9 ....
Conversation B ⊙ 10 ....

2 Look at the *audioscript* of conversations A and B. What questions do the speakers ask to

a start a conversation? ....
....
b keep a conversation going? ....
....
....
....

Focus on ...
ab**C**def
questions to start conversations

Look at this question from conversation B. Notice how one part is positive and the other is negative. Look at the order of the words in each part. The first part is a statement but the second part is a question.

It's cold today,   isn't it?
        statement   question

Match the two parts of the questions.
a It isn't 12 o'clock already,   don't they?
b It's nice food,   is it?
c They look good,   does he?
d She's from Taiwan,   isn't it?
e He doesn't look happy,   isn't she?

Speak up!

3 Ask a question like the ones in *Focus on* to start a conversation at a party.

What questions could you ask to keep the conversation going? Use the *Speaking strategy* to help you.

4 ⊙ 11 You meet new people at a party. Listen and answer their questions.

Class bonus

Imagine you are at a party. Walk around the room and have conversations with people about the weather, their interests etc. Start a conversation and ask questions to keep it going. Try and talk to everyone in the class.

E xtra practice

Telephone a friend in English and invite them to do something with you at the weekend. You could also listen to how people keep conversations going in English. Listen to conversations on TV or in public places like the bus. Record any new words in your vocabulary notebook.

Can-do checklist

Tick what you can do.

	Can do	Need more practice
I can make and answer invitations.	✔	✔
I can start conversations.		
I can take part in 'small talk' conversations.		

Unit **2**

I'm phoning about the house

go to Useful language p. 78

Get ready to listen and speak

● Read the accommodation advertisements and match them to the pictures.

1

2

3

A

> **GLEN EDEN** 2 brm
> house near shopping
> centre and train.
> $270 tel 483-86152

B

> **GLEN EDEN** 3 brm f/f
> house with garage, garden;
> $330pw inc bills. Phone
> 915-33291, 0273 463-1106

C

> **GREY LYNN** 1 brm apt,
> close to shopping centre;
> $190pw, n/s only.
> Ph 485 63142

● The places above are all in Auckland, New Zealand. Which place would you like to live in? Why?

A Listening – Phoning a landlord

1 ● 🔊12 **Listen to Susan telephoning a landlord. Which advertisement in *Get ready* is she phoning about?**

Learning tip

Read the exercise before you listen and make sure you know what you are listening for. For example, is it a number or a word?

2 ● 🔊12 **Read Susan's notes on the right. Then listen again and complete the gaps.
(mins = minutes)**

Did you know …?

These are some common abbreviations in newspaper advertisements.

brm/bed = bedroom	f/f = fully furnished
pw = per week	inc = including
apt = apartment	n/s = non smoker
min = minimum	tel/ph= telephone

People say 'flat' in the UK and 'apartment' in the US. 'Unit' is used in New Zealand and Australia. This is a small house attached to one or more similar houses.

Address: House number: ᵃ __36__

ᵇ ----------------------------- Street

Close to – shops: ᶜ _____ mins walk

— train station: ᵈ _____ mins walk

Two bedrooms: both double bedrooms? ᵉYES / NO

Large garden: ᶠYES / NO

Visit flat at ᵍ _____ pm.

B Speaking – Phoning a landlord

Speaking strategy
Checking information

1 Look at part of the conversation Susan had. What does Susan say when she checks the address?

Does she ask a question?

YES / NO

Susan: Ah hello … I'm phoning about the house in Glen Eden that's advertised in the paper today.
Landlord: Yes.
Susan: I was just wondering where it is.
Landlord: 36 Arawa Street …
Susan: Sorry, 36 …
Landlord: Arawa Street, A-R-A-W-A. It's number 36.
Susan: Oh OK …

2 ◆13 Now listen to Susan. What happens to Susan's voice when she checks the address? Choose the correct answer.

a It goes down.
b It stays the same.

You need to listen carefully to the way people's voices go up and down to express meaning. This is intonation.

3 ◆14 Listen to other ways of checking information. Does the intonation rise or fall? Put an arrow ↗ or ↘.

 What was that?

 Pardon?

Speak up!

4 ◆15 Listen to the landlord and use the *Speaking strategy* to check some of the information.

Example: a
Landlord: The other bedroom probably only fits a single bed.
You say: Sorry, the other bedroom fits a …

a Check the size of one of the bedrooms.
  Landlord: The other bedroom probably only fits a single bed.
b Check what is ten minutes' walk away.
  Landlord: Um, it's probably about a ten-minute walk to the shops.
  You: --
c Check what time the landlord will be at the house.
  Landlord: OK, if you're interested I'll be down there at 5.30.
  You: --

5 ◆16 Listen and practise the intonation used to check the information.

Focus on …
asking questions

1 Look at the questions Susan asked. Which is more polite? Tick ✓ a or b.
  a I was just wondering where it is. ☐
  b What size are they? ☐

2 Look at the questions again. What is different about the word order?
  I was just wondering   where   it   is
                    question word + subject + verb

    What size   are   they?
  question word + verb + subject

3 Change the questions below so they are more polite.
  a How far is it? I was just wondering how far it is.
  ----
  b How much is it? ---
  ----
  c How many bedrooms are there? -----------------------
  ----
  d When can I move in? --------------------------------------
  ----

When you talk to someone you don't know very well, e.g. a landlord, you should ask polite questions.

Sound smart
Sentence stress

1 ◆17 Listen to this question and underline the main stress.
  I was just wondering where it is.

  Notice how *was* and *just* are not stressed so they become /wəz/ and /dʒəs/.

2 ◆17 Listen and repeat the question.
  I was just wondering where it is.

3 ◆18 Practise saying these questions. Then repeat them after the speaker.
  a I was just wondering how far it is.
  b I was just wondering how much it is.
  c I was just wondering how many bedrooms there are.
  d I was just wondering when I can move in.

Try and use these unstressed forms when you speak. It will make you sound more natural.

C Listening – A problem in the house

A few weeks later Susan has a problem in her flat. She phones her landlord.

1 🔘 19 **Listen to the conversation. What is the problem?**

----

2 🔘 19 **Listen again and answer the questions below.**

a When did the problem start?

----

b Has Susan tried to fix the problem?

----

c What will the landlord try to do?

----

d When will the landlord visit Susan's flat?

D Speaking – A problem in the house

Speaking strategy
Complaints and solutions

1 Match the problems 1–4 to the solutions a–d.

1 I've lost my key and I can't get inside. __b__
2 The shower's broken so I can't wash. _____
3 The lights aren't working so I can't see. _____
4 There's a hole in the roof and the rain's coming in. _____

a send a plumber
b get a new one made
c send a builder
d send an electrician

2 🎧 **20 Listen to Susan leaving an answerphone message for her landlord about another problem. <u>Underline</u> the problem and ⟨circle⟩ the solution she suggests.**

> Hello, it's Susan from your flat in Arawa Street. I'm phoning to let you know there's a broken window. We can't close it and it's really cold! Could you please send someone around to fix it? Thanks. Bye.

When something goes wrong you explain the problem and suggest a solution. Look at the other example on the right.

Speak up!

3 🎧 **21 Choose one of the problems in Exercise 1. Phone your landlord and leave a message on his answerphone. Describe the problem and suggest a solution. Listen to the landlord's answerphone message. Start like this**

Hi it's (say your name) from your flat in Arawa Street.

4 Choose another problem from the pictures in Exercise 1 or think of a new one and leave another message for the landlord.

Problem

> Susan says:
> We've got a bit of a problem in the flat. The oven isn't working.
>
> Other expressions:
> I'm phoning to let you know / tell you that the oven is broken.

Solution

> Susan says:
> I was wondering if you could get someone to come and have a look at it for us.
>
> Other expressions:
> Would it be possible to get someone to fix it? Could you please get an electrician to come round?

Learning tip

Talking on the telephone can be difficult because you can't see who you are talking to.
To make it easier you can:
– think about what you will say and how you will say it before you talk on the telephone.
– think about what the other person might say before you telephone them.
– repeat part of an answer to check you understand.
– ask the speaker to repeat things you don't understand and to spell difficult names and addresses.

Class bonus

Work with a partner and role play the conversations between the landlord and the tenant. When you have finished, change roles.

E ✗ tra practice

Telephone a rental agency that rents houses and flats to English speakers. Ask them about places to rent in an area you would like to live in.
Or go to www.gumtree.com and choose a city. Look at the advertisements. Can you find any more abbreviations?

Can-do checklist

Tick what you can do.

	Can do	Need more practice
I can check I have understood information correctly.	✔	✔
I can ask polite questions to find out information.		
I can describe a problem and suggest a solution.		

Unit 3
How do I buy a ticket?

go to Useful language p. 79

Get ready to listen and speak

- Tick ✓ the transport you have used:
  - helicopter ☐
  - ferry ☐
  - tram ☐
  - hovercraft ☐
  - motorbike ☐

- What do visitors need to know before catching a bus or a train in your city or town? What can you tell them? Think about the questions below.
  What public transport is there?
  Where can you buy tickets?
  What different kinds of tickets are there?
  Where do you show your ticket?

A Listening – Getting information

Matt has just arrived in Osaka, Japan. He wants to get around by public transport. Kumiko, an Information Officer, helps him.

1 🔊22 Listen to their conversation. Tick ✓ the information that Matt asks about.

   a train timetables ☐
   b ticket machines ☐
   c late night train services ☐
   d ticket prices ☐
   e train and bus connections ☐

2 🔊22 Read the instructions for using the Osaka underground. Listen again and complete the gaps with the word or number you hear.

⏩ Paying for tickets

You can use these coins in all ticket machines: 500 yen, ᵃ___100___ yen, ᵇ_____ yen, 10 yen.

You can use these notes in all ticket machines: ᶜ_____ yen.

You can use these notes in some, but not all ticket machines: ᵈ_____ yen and 10,000 yen.

Ticket prices can be found on the big ᵉ_____ above the machine.

3 Try to remember what you heard. Are these sentences true (T) or false (F)?

a When you go through the ticket gate, put your ticket in the machine. ....

b Take the ticket with you when get on the train. ....

c When you arrive at your destination somebody will take your ticket.

....

Did you know ...?

The London Underground is known as 'the tube'. In the US people call underground trains 'the subway'.

Focus on ... saying numbers

ab**c**def

🎧 **123** Listen to how these numbers are said. Tick ✓ a or b.

1 250
  a two hundred fifty ☐
  b two hundred and fifty ☐

2 5200
  a five thousand two hundred ☐
  b five thousand and two hundred ☐

3 5250
  a five thousand and two hundred fifty ☐
  b five thousand two hundred and fifty ☐

4 1000
  a a thousand ☐
  b one thousand ☐

In American English people say two hundred fifty, but in British English people say two hundred and fifty.

B Speaking – Getting information

Speaking strategy
Asking for information

Matt uses these questions to ask for information:

a **How will I know** which notes I can use?

b **How can I tell** how much money I need to put in a machine?

c **What should I do** next?

d Then **what do I do**?

1 Some of the questions ask about an action and some ask about understanding. Put the questions in the correct box. Two of them have been done for you.

Understanding	Actions
a How will I know which notes I can use?	c What should I do next?
....	....
....	....

Speak up!

2 Look at the conversations below. Read what Kumiko says and think about what you will say. Use the words to make questions like the ones in *Speaking strategy*.

Example: a
Kumiko: Some ticket machines take both notes and coins.
You say: How will I know if a machine takes both?
Kumiko: It will say on the machine.

a You: how / know / machine takes both?

b Kumiko: You put the money in the machine.
  You: how / know / correct ticket price?
  Kumiko: You can see on the map.

c Kumiko: You get the ticket from the machine.
  You: then what / do?
  Kumiko: Go to the ticket gate.

d Kumiko: You put the ticket in the machine.
  You: what / do next?
  Kumiko: Remember to take it when it comes out of the machine.

e Kumiko: You can use credit cards in some stations.
  You: how / tell / machine takes credit cards?
  Kumiko: It will say on the machine.

3 🎧 124 Now talk to Kumiko and ask her your questions.

C Listening – Asking more questions

1 ◉ 📀 25 **Listen to the rest of the conversation. Matt asks about two of the following. Tick ✓ them.**

a train timetables ☐   c multi-trip tickets ☐
b discount cards ☐   d directions to a station ☐

2 ◉ 📀 25 **Read the sentences below about the 'No-My-Car-Day' Pass and the Rainbow Card. Listen again and place the letter in the correct box. One sentence matches both cards. You may want to listen more than once.**

a You can use it every Friday.
b You can buy one for 5,000 yen.
c You can buy it on the 20th of every month.
d You get a discount with it.
e You don't get a discount with it.
f You can use it for more than one trip.
g You can use it for one day.

Note: 'No-My-Car-Day' is not a standard English expression.

No-My-Car-Day Pass
-------------- a --------------

Rainbow Card

D Speaking – Asking more questions

Speaking strategy
Asking about one thing or another

Matt wants to check some information about the discount card.

> Do I get this discount pass from normal ticket machines or from special ticket machines?

1 **Underline the word which joins two ideas together. Is it necessary to repeat the verb in the second part of the sentence?**

YES/NO

Sound smart
Stress and intonation on one thing or another

1 ◉ 📀 26 Listen to Matt's question again and <u>underline</u> the two words which are strongly stressed.
Do I get this discount pass from normal ticket machines or from special ticket machines?

Listen and repeat. Make sure your voice goes up and down like Matt's.

This stress and intonation make it clear that Matt is asking a question.

Learning tip

When you hear new expressions or questions, make sure you listen for the words or syllables that are stressed. When you record these words in your notebook, mark the stress by <u>underlining</u> the strongest syllable, e.g. ma<u>chines</u>.

Speak up!

2 🔊27 **Listen to questions a–g below and repeat them. Use the words below to help you. Make sure you stress the correct words and that your voice goes up in the first part of the question and down in the second part.**

Example: a
You say: Do I buy a Rainbow Card from a normal machine or a special machine?

a I buy / Rainbow Card from / normal machine / special machine?
b I buy / discount card from all stations / only some stations?
c I buy / Rainbow Card only on Monday / any day?
d I buy / 500 yen card / 1000 yen card?
e I get / discount of 200 yen / 250 yen?
f I use / Rainbow Card at / usual ticket gate / special ticket gate?

3 🔊28 **You visit Osaka and ask Kumiko for information. Read her answers and think about what you will say. Use the words below to help you. Then talk to Kumiko and find out about train tickets.**

Example: a
You say: Where are the ticket machines?
Kumiko: They're near all the stations.

a where / ticket machines?
b You: 10,000 yen notes? _____
   Kumiko: Yes, you can use them in some machines.
c You: how / which notes? _____
   Kumiko: It will say on the machine.
d You: a discount ticket? _____
   Kumiko: Yes, you can buy a No-My-Car-Day discount ticket on Fridays.
e You: every Friday / some Fridays? _____
   Kumiko: Every Friday and on the 20th of every month.

Class bonus

Do a class survey on public transport. If you come from different countries, ask each other questions about public transport in your country. If you come from the same country, ask each other about how often you use public transport and what different tickets you buy. Go around the class and ask and answer questions.

E X tra practice

You can practise similar conversations with a friend. Go to the Transport for London website: http://www.tfl.gov.uk
Read the information about travel tickets, then role play a conversation between a tourist and an Information Officer.

Can-do checklist

Tick what you can do.

	Can do	Need more practice
I can understand important information about public transport.	✓	✓
I can ask for travel information.		
I can check my understanding of information.		

Unit 4
Shall we go out for dinner?

Get ready to listen and speak

- Think about the questions below.
  What's your favourite food?
  Are you a good cook?
  What's the last thing you ate?

  Do you prefer restaurants or take-aways?
  What do you usually eat for breakfast?
  Have you tried food from other countries?

go to Useful language p. 79

A Listening – Going out for dinner

Neil and Rachel have just got home from work and are talking about what to have for dinner.

1 🔊 29 **Listen to their conversation. Tick ✓ the food they talk about and circle the kind of restaurant they decide to go to.**

Cambodian ☐
Chinese ☐
Thai ☐
Indian ☐
Japanese ☐
Vietnamese ☐

Learning tip

Sometimes it's possible to remember information from the first time you listened. Check this information when you listen for the second time.

2 **Read the questions in Exercise 3 below. How many can you answer before you listen?**

3 🔊 29 **Now listen again and answer the questions.**

a Why do Rachel and Neil want to go out?
  They are too tired to cook dinner.
b Why don't they want to go to a Thai restaurant?
  ----
c Where is the new Cambodian restaurant?
  ----
d Does Cambodian food have a stronger flavour than Thai food?
  ----
e How expensive is the Cambodian restaurant?

Did you know ...?

Fifty per cent of British people eat fish and chips once a month and there are over 10,000 fish and chip shops in the UK. However, a recent survey revealed that the favourite food in the UK is chicken tikka masala.

B Speaking – Going out for dinner

Speaking strategy
Making suggestions

1 During the conversation in Listening A, Rachel and Neil talk about their ideas.

a So **shall we** go out for dinner?

b **What about** having Thai food?

c **We could** try that for a change.

d **I've got an idea.**

e **Let's** try that then.

The expressions in bold are useful when you want to make a suggestion.

Which expression is followed by *–ing*? Can any of the other expressions also be followed by *–ing*?

YES/NO

Sound smart
Intonation of suggestions

1 ●30 Listen to the three suggestions. For each one, tick ✓ the pattern you hear, a or b.

a Shall we go out for dinner? ☐   b Shall we go out for dinner? ☐

a What about going out for dinner? ☐   b What about going out for dinner? ☐

a We could go out for dinner. ☐   b We could go out for dinner. ☐

2 The intonation in these examples rises. Listen and decide why.

----

3 ●30 Listen and repeat the three suggestions. Make sure you copy Neil's intonation.

Speak up!

2 Use the word in **bold** and the verb to make a suggestion about dinner.

Example: a
You say: Shall we go to a French restaurant for dinner?

a French restaurant **shall** / go
b salad / **let's** / have
c Chinese restaurant / **about** / go
d pizza / **could** / have
e Turkish restaurant / **let's** / go
f sushi / **shall** / eat
g roast chicken / **about** / have
h Mexican restaurant / **could** / try

Restaurant

Los Sombreros

C Listening – Talking about a meal

1 🔘 **31** **Neil tells you about his meal at the Khmer Café. Listen and number the words in the box. Write 1 by the things he ate for a starter. Write 2 by the things he ate for a main course. Put a cross ✗ by the things he does not talk about.**

chicken	noodles	lime leaves ......
mushroom soup ..1..	egg	chicken curry parcel ..2..
curry	beef	fish sauce ......
ginger	tomatoes	lemon grass ......
coriander	coconut milk	mushroom ......
rice		

2 🔘 **32** **Rachel tells you about her meal. Listen and correct six mistakes below. The first mistake is corrected for you.**

> I went to the Khmer Café for dinner on Friday. For a starter, I had shrimp ~~curry~~ ^soup^. There was a taste of coconut and lime. It was quite sweet. Then for a main course I had vegetable stir-fry. It's made with pineapple and tomatoes. This dish was very mild. For a dessert I had fried bananas and honey. It was OK.

Learning tip

Sometimes it's important to listen very carefully and understand every word. Listening to a short text like this can help you practise listening for details, but it's not a good idea to listen to a long conversation in this way.

D Speaking – Talking about a meal

Speaking strategy
Telling people what you ate

1 For each dish they ate Neil and Rachel talk about four things:

a the ingredients
b their opinion
c if the dish was a starter, a main course or a dessert
d the name of the dish

Look at the *audioscript*.
What order does Neil say these things?

What order does Rachel say these things?

----

2 When we talk about different courses we use the following expressions:

> For a starter I had …

> For a main course I had …

> For dessert I had …

Do we use the word *course* with the words *starter* and *dessert*?

Can we put *a* before *dessert*?

When we talk about a dish, we usually say which course and the name of the dish first. We give our opinion and the ingredients in either order.

Note: In New Zealand and Australia, you can say *for a main*. You don't need to say *course*.

Speak up!

3 **Imagine you ate these meals. Use the information below to talk about what you ate.**

Example: a

You say: Last night I went to an Italian restaurant. For a main course, I had spaghetti bolognese. It was very good. It's made with beef and tomatoes.

a

restaurant	part of meal	dish	opinion	ingredients
Italian	main	spaghetti bolognese	very good	beef and tomatoes

b

restaurant	part of meal	dish	opinion	ingredients
Japanese	starter	miso soup	tasty	tofu and onion

c

restaurant	part of meal	dish	opinion	ingredients
Spanish	main	paella	full of flavour	seafood and rice

d

restaurant	part of meal	dish	opinion	ingredients
Chinese	main	beef stir-fry	quite spicy	broccoli and ginger

e

restaurant	part of meal	dish	opinion	ingredients
French	dessert	crème brulée	really sweet	vanilla and cream

f

restaurant	part of meal	dish	opinion	ingredients
Turkish	main	shish kebab	delicious	lamb and peppers

4 🔊 **33 Think about the last time you went to a restaurant. Listen and answer the questions.**

a When did you last go to a restaurant?
b What type of restaurant was it?
c Did you have a starter? What was it?
d Did you have a dessert? What was it?
e What did you eat for the main course?
f What's it made with?
g Did you enjoy it?

Class bonus

In groups, design a restaurant menu. Think about what type of restaurant it is and include starters, main courses and desserts. Remember to talk in English!

E X tra practice

The English Language Listening Lab Online has short listening exercises on different topics. Go to http://www.elllo.org
Search for 'food' to get a list of exercises about food. Click on 'play slide show' to listen. You can usually read an audioscript of the exercise after you have heard it, and sometimes there are comprehension questions too.

Can-do checklist

Tick what you can do.

	Can do	Need more practice
I can make suggestions.	✓	✓
I can understand descriptions of food and meals.		
I can talk about what I ate in a restaurant.		

Unit5
You should go to the police

Get ready to **listen and speak**

- You are lost in a strange city. Which of the following would you do? Tick ✓ them.
  buy a map ☐
  ask someone in a shop ☐
  phone a friend ☐
  ask a policeman ☐
  keep walking ☐

  What would you do first? Why?

- You leave your wallet on a train when you are abroad. Which of the following would you do? Tick ✓ them.
  phone the railway station ☐
  go to the police station ☐
  go to your embassy ☐
  phone your insurance company ☐
  phone your family ☐

  What would you do first? Why?

  ----

go to Useful language p. 79

A Listening – Saying what happened

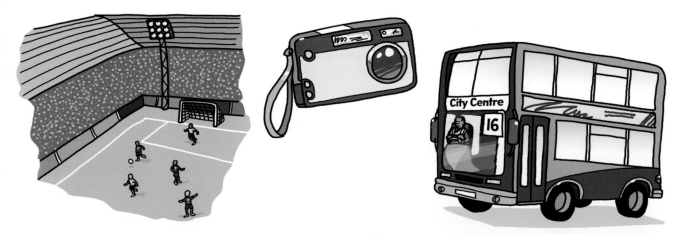

1 🔘 34 **Arnaud is studying English in Birmingham. He talks to his teacher, David, about the weekend. Look at the pictures above. What do you think happened? Listen and check your ideas.**

2 🔘 34 **Listen again. Are the sentences below true (T) or false? (F) Correct the ones which are false.**
   a Arnaud had a ~~good~~ bad weekend. _F_
   b Arnaud lost his camera at the football match. ......
   c Arnaud went to the bus company office. ......
   d David thinks it's a good idea to go to the police. ......
   e Arnaud decides to tell the police about his missing camera. ......
   f David offers to go to the police station with Arnaud. ......
   g They will go to the police immediately. ......

> **Learning tip**
>
> When you check your answers, think about why you got them right or wrong. If you know why you got something wrong, maybe you won't make the same mistake again.

B Speaking – Saying what happened

Speaking strategy
Avoiding repetition

1 **Look at these extracts from David and Arnaud's conversation. Listen again and circle what they actually said.**

a David: Did you get it back?
   Arnaud: *No, I didn't. / No, I didn't get it back.*

b Arnaud: Well I'm free now. *Are you free? / Are you?*
   David: I have to go to the bank …

2 **Choose two reasons why David and Arnaud leave out words.**

a They are lazy and don't want to repeat information.
b It's not necessary to repeat information.
c They don't know what to say.
d It helps the conversation move naturally.

Speak up!

3 **Arnaud and David talk again later. Look at part of their conversation and complete the gaps with an expression from the box.**

I'd like to	~~yours~~	I haven't	I didn't	Did you	it

David: And how was the rest of your weekend, Arnaud?
Arnaud: Not bad thanks. How was ª_____yours_____?
David: Good. I went out for dinner with some friends on Saturday. I heard there was a free concert in the park, but I didn't go. ᵇ_____?
Arnaud: No, ᶜ_____ . It was too cold. I went to the movies instead.
David: Oh yeah. What did you see?
Arnaud: *Star Wars*. They were showing the second one. It was great. Have you seen ᵈ_____ ?
David: No, ᵉ_____ but ᶠ_____ . I've only seen the first one.

🔊 **835 Now listen and check your answers.**

4 🔊 **836 Imagine you are Arnaud. Cover the conversation above and talk to David. Use the words below to help you.**

David: And how was the rest of your weekend, Arnaud?
Arnaud: not bad. yours?
You: Not bad thanks. How was yours?

David: Good. I went out for dinner with some friends on Saturday. I heard there was a free concert in the park, but I didn't go. Did you?
Arnaud: no / cold.   go / movies.
You: --

David: Oh yeah. What did you see?
Arnaud: Star Wars. show / second one. great. you / see / it?
You: --

David: No, I haven't but I'd like to. I've only seen the first one.

5 🔊 **837 Listen and answer the questions about you. Try not to repeat unnecessary words.**

a How was your weekend?
b What was the last movie you saw?
c What was it like?
d When did you last go on holiday?
e Who did you go with?
f Did you have a good time?

Sound smart
Pronunciation of *did you*

🔊 **838 Listen to this question.**
Did you get it back?

Notice how *did you* is pronounced /dɪdʒə/. Listen again and repeat the question.

1 Ask questions using the words below. Remember to pronounce *did you* as /dɪdʒə/.
  Example: a
  You say: Did you have a good weekend?

a have / good weekend?
b what / do?
c go / cinema?
d what / see?
e like / the film?
f go / with friends?
🔊 **839 Listen and check.**

2 🔊 **840 Listen and underline the sentence stress.**
  I did.   I didn't.

3 🔊 **841 Listen to the questions and answer *Yes, I did* or *No, I didn't*. Remember to stress *did*.**

Learning tip

To help keep a conversation going, don't just answer questions, make sure you ask them too, like David and Arnaud do.

C Listening – At the police station

Owner's first names: _Arnaud_____ Surname: ª _Lafayette___
Street: ᵇ_____
Town/city: _Birmingham_____ Postcode: ᶜ_____
Mobile phone: ᵈ_____
Email: ᵉ_____

Where property lost/stolen:
ᶠ_____

When:
ᵍ_____

Insurance claim ☑ Yes ☐ No

Description of property:
small ʰ   _camera_____
grey ⁱ   _with shoulder strap_____
_Nikon_____
not very ʲ_____
_name inside_____

Arnaud and David go to the police station. The police officer asks Arnaud some questions.

1 Look at part of the police officer's form. Some information is missing. Can you complete any of it before you listen?

2 🔘 42 Now listen and complete the form.

Did you know …?

This is how we say telephone numbers and email addresses:

0 *oh* or *zero*   33 *three three* or *double three*
333 *treble* or *triple 3*   / *slash*
aaa *lower case*   @ *at*
AAA *upper case*   . *dot*

D Speaking – At the police station

Speaking strategy
Describing things

1 Look at the *audioscript* on page 92. What questions does the police officer ask to get information about Arnaud's camera?

a Can you _____?
b What's _____?
c Do you _____?

Look at how Arnaud describes his camera. He gives a general description first.

> It's quite a **small digital** camera.

Then he gives more detail using the expressions below.

It's in …
with …
It's a …
It's not very …
It's got …

> It's in a **grey case** with a **shoulder strap**. It's a **Nikon**. It's **not very old**. And it's got **my name inside**.

2 Complete the table with the words in bold Arnaud uses to describe his camera.

Size	Colour	Age	Brand	Type	Other
small				digital	

Learning tip

It's a good idea to record new words in categories like the table above. It helps you to remember them and you can easily add other words to the lists.

Speak up!

3 Put the words in the box into the table above.

silver   sports   brown   Nokia   woman's   red   three years old
Gucci   hard case   quite old   black handles   black   new   big

4 Use the words in the table to describe these things.

a

b

c

d

You say: It's a woman's
watch. It's small
and silver.

5 Describe something that is special to you. Start with a general description and then give more detail.

Example:
You say: I have a brown leather wallet. It's very old and it's got some photos inside.

Class bonus

Work with a partner and role play the situation at the police station.
A: You are the police officer.
Ask questions to find out what happened.
B: Something you own was lost or stolen. Describe the object and what happened.

Extra practice

Telephone a bus or train company in your city. In English, ask them what they do with lost property.

Can-do checklist

Tick what you can do.

	Can do	Need more practice
I can speak without repeating unnecessary words.	✓	✓
I can understand information about personal details and events.		
I can give general and detailed descriptions.		

Unit 6
Have you got a headache?

Get ready to listen and speak

○ How are these people feeling? Match the pictures to the expressions.
1 I've got a terrible headache. __d__
2 My throat is really sore. _____
3 I can't stop sneezing. _____
4 I've got a temperature. _____
5 I've got a bad cough. _____
6 I've got sore eyes. _____
7 I've got a swollen knee. _____

When we have an illness, we talk about our symptoms,
e.g. sneezing is a symptom of a cold.

go to Useful language p. 79

go to Useful language p. 79

A Listening – At the chemist's

Chu Hua thinks she has the flu so she goes to the chemist.

1 🔘 43 Listen to the conversation. What symptoms does she have?

a _____
b _____
c _____

2 🔘 43 Look at these instructions for different medicines. Listen again and complete the gaps.

Did you know …?

Chemist and *pharmacy* are used in British English but *drugstore* is used in American English.

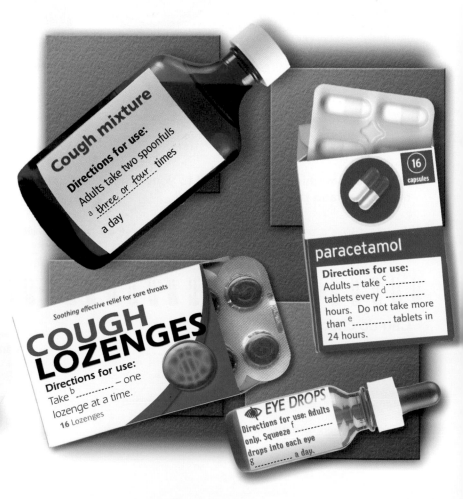

Cough mixture
Directions for use:
Adults take two spoonfuls
a _three or four_ times
a day

16 capsules

paracetamol
Directions for use:
Adults – take c _____
tablets every d _____
hours. Do not take more
than e _____ tablets in
24 hours.

Soothing effective relief for sore throats
COUGH LOZENGES
Directions for use:
Take b _____ – one
lozenge at a time.
16 Lozenges

EYE DROPS
Directions for use: Adults
only. Squeeze f _____
drops into each eye
g _____ a day.

B Speaking – At the chemist's

Speaking strategy
Giving instructions

1 Read what the pharmacist said and put the expressions in bold into the correct column. The first one has been done for you.

> **Don't take** it just when you've got a cough because then it takes a little while to work. **You need to take** it before you cough.

> **You should take** paracetamol for your headache.

> **Take** two of those every four hours.

What to do	What not to do
	Don't take

2 **Look at the *audioscript* on page 92 and find three more expressions to add to the table.**

Sound smart
Sentence stress for instructions and advice

1 • 44 Listen to the sentences and <u>underline</u> the word which is stressed the most. The first one has been done for you.

You need to <u>take</u> it before you cough.
You should take paracetamol.
Don't take it when you cough.
You shouldn't take it for longer than that.
You mustn't take more than that.

2 What pattern can you see in the word stress of these sentences?

3 • 44 Listen to the sentences again and practise saying them.

Learning tip

It's a good idea to practise describing the situation and think about what people might ask you before you have to say it, for example, at the chemist's / post office / bank etc.

Speak up!

3 **Match the symptoms with the remedies.**

Symptoms	Remedies
toothache	cough mixture
sore throat	painkillers
swollen knee	drops
sore eyes	lozenges
cough	ice

4 • 45 **Listen to six people tell you what is wrong with them. Give them instructions using the expressions in *Speaking strategy*. Use a different expression each time. To sound more helpful you can say *Oh no … It/They will help*.**

Example: a
You hear: I've got a terrible toothache.
You say: Oh no. You should take some painkillers. They will help.

a toothache

b a sore throat
You: ....

c swollen knee
You: ....

d sore eyes
You: ....

e headache
You: ....

f cough
You: ....

C Listening – Home remedies

1 When people are not feeling well, they sometimes use home remedies.
Match each picture to the correct ingredient.

1 honey _b_   2 garlic _____   3 Chinese radish _____   4 herbal tea _____   5 lemon _____

2 🔵**46** Listen to three people from Saudi Arabia, Japan and Brazil talk about home remedies. Tick ✓ the ingredients each person talks about.

	Chinese radish	garlic	camomile	honey	lemon
a Ali			✓		
b Seiji					
c Ana					

3 🔵**46** Listen again and put one word in each gap.

Ali:

In Saudi Arabia what you do if you have the ª _____ _flu_ _____ is you drink babunej. It's a kind of hot drink. It's made with camomile, which is a herb. You drink it very ᵇ _____ and you sometimes have it with lots of ᶜ _____ . You get vitamin C from that.

Seiji:

In Japan if you have a ᵈ_____ _____, we use daikon, a Chinese radish. It's a bit like a large white ᵉ_____ . We grind the Chinese radish and put honey on it and leave it for a while. Then we wait until the ᶠ_____ comes out and then we ᵍ_____ it.

Ana:

In Brazil if you're not well, you've got a cold or flu or something like that, well garlic is really important. You have a glass of ʰ_____ and you put a little garlic in it and mix it together. Every ⁱ_____ _____ , you drink ʲ_____ or ᵏ_____ spoonfuls of the liquid. I don't know if it works but we try it.

D Speaking – Home remedies

Speaking strategy
Describing what something is

1 **Look at C Listening Exercise 3. How do the speakers describe what something is? Complete the expressions below.**

   a It's a .... of hot drink.
   b It's made with camomile, ... is a herb.
   c It's a bit .... a large white carrot.

2 **Seiji says *We use daikon, a Chinese radish*. Is it also correct to say *We use daikon, which is a Chinese radish*?**

   YES / NO

Speak up!

3 **Here are some other things people use when they don't feel well. Match the ingredients in A to a description in B.**

A	B
ginger	small orange
hot lemon juice	cream
mandarins	drink
vapour rub	herb

4 **Describe the ingredients in A using the expressions in *Speaking strategy*. Use these verbs to help you.**

   eat (x2)   make   use

   You say: You should eat some ginger. It's a bit like a herb.

5 **Explain a home remedy from your country. Use the expressions in *Speaking strategy* to help you describe the ingredients.**

Class bonus

Discuss these questions in groups. In your country, how popular are home remedies? Is modern medicine more popular? Do you prefer to use home remedies or modern medicine? Why?

Extra practice

If you are in an English-speaking country, go to the chemist's and ask them about home remedies. Are they popular?

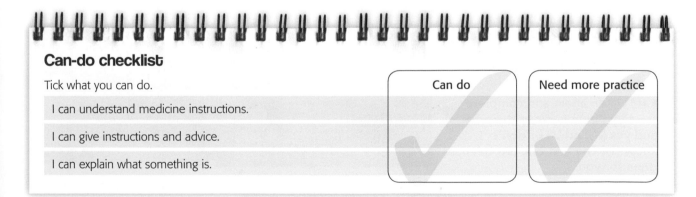

Can-do checklist

Tick what you can do.

	Can do	Need more practice
I can understand medicine instructions.	✔	✔
I can give instructions and advice.		
I can explain what something is.		

Unit 7
How about a hostel?

Get ready to listen and speak

○ Match the accommodation in 1 to 4 to the correct description. The first one has been done for you.

1 guesthouse

2 campsite

3 hostel

4 hotel

a You usually sleep in a large room with other guests, sometimes called a dorm. There is often a kitchen so you can make your own meals and sometimes there's a bar.

b You have your own room and usually your own bathroom too. Breakfast is often included in the price and you can sometimes have other meals too.

c These are sometimes called 'bed and breakfasts'. This is usually a private house where you get your own room. Breakfast is usually included and sometimes all meals are included too. Sometimes you have to share a bathroom.

d You sleep in a tent here. There are usually toilets and showers. Sometimes there are shops.

○ Which of the places above do you think is the cheapest? Which is the most expensive? Put them in order.

cheapest   most expensive

---------------------------   -------------------------   -------------------------   ---------------------------

go to Useful language p. 79

A Listening – At the Tourist Information Centre

Anke is a German tourist. She has just arrived in Vancouver and is looking for accommodation. She goes to the Tourist Information Office.

1 🔊 **47** Listen to the conversation between Anke and Dan, the Tourist Information Officer. Tick ✓ the types of accommodation in *Get ready* that they talk about.

2 🔊 **47** Listen again and complete the table below. Write the price and yes (✓), no (✗) or don't know (?). The first one has been done for you.

Place	Price ($)	Share room	Share bathroom	Breakfast
The Pioneer	2.00	✗	✗	✓
The Vancouver Inn				
BC Lodge				
The Maple Leaf Villa				

Did you know …?

Dollars ($) are used in Canada, the US, Australia and New Zealand. A slang term for dollars is *bucks* (20 dollars = 20 bucks). Pounds (£) are used in the UK. A slang term for pounds is *quid* (20 pounds = 20 quid).

B Speaking – At the Tourist Information Centre

Speaking strategy
Asking about accommodation

1 Anke uses different expressions to get more information about accommodation. Put them in the table below. The first one has been done for you. There are two expressions for each.

a I'm looking for somewhere to stay.
b Can you recommend somewhere central?
c It's too expensive for me.
d What's it like?
e I'm not keen on sharing a bedroom.
f That sounds interesting.
g Can you tell me more about that?
h Could I have a look at it?

making a general enquiry	a
asking for more detailed information	
saying 'no'	
showing interest	

2 The sentences below are from Exercise 1. Replace the words *in italics* with an expression from the box.

| cooking my own breakfast   really good |
| far from the centre |

a It's too *expensive for me.*

---

b I'm not keen on *sharing a bedroom.*

---

c That sounds *interesting.*

Now complete these expressions.

| sleeping in a tent   far from the airport   great |

d It's too _____
e I'm not keen on _____
f That sounds _____

Learning tip

When you learn a new expression, it's a good idea to practise it with different words, like in Exercise 2.

Sound smart
Word stress

1 🔘 **48** Listen to the word stress in *noisy* and *quiet*. Which syllable is stressed? ....

2 🔘 **49** Repeat these words and mark the stress. Which word has different stress from the others?
noisy   quiet   hotel   central   luggage   private   hostel

3 Where do you think the stress is in these three-syllable words?
expensive   convenient   interesting   possible

4 🔘 **50** Listen and check. Then listen again and repeat the words.

Learning tip

When you look up a new word in the dictionary, remember to check which syllable is stressed. A ' is put in front of the stressed syllable e.g. noisy /ˈnɔɪzi/. This means the stress is on the first syllable.

Speak up!

3 🔘 **51** Listen to Dan speak then use the words below to help you answer his questions. Choose one of the three words or expressions *in italics*.

Example: a
Dan: Hello. Can I help you?
You say: I'm looking for somewhere cheap.

a Dan: Hello. Can I help you?
  You: looking / somewhere / *cheap/quiet/private*
b Dan: Hi there. How can I help you?
  You: looking / somewhere / *central/inexpensive/ convenient*
c Dan: How about the Vancouver Inn? It's $110 a night.
  You: too *expensive/far from the centre/close to the airport.*
d Dan: You could try a hostel.
  You: not keen on *sharing a bedroom/cooking my own meals/staying somewhere noisy*
e Dan: How about this guesthouse – the Maple Leaf Villa? It's very central, but it's not too expensive.
  You: sounds / *interesting/possible/good*

4 Now try to do Exercise 3 again with this book closed.

C Listening – The guesthouse

You go to the Maple Leaf Villa and talk to Ray, the owner.

1 🔊 52 **Ray shows you four different rooms in the guesthouse. Listen and write the rooms he shows you.**

Room 1 ......*lounge*......
Room 2 ....
Room 3 ....
Room 4 ....

2 🔊 52 **Listen again and write down what is in each room.**

Room	Feature
1	widescreen TV
2	
3	
4	

3 🔊 52 **Listen again and answer these questions.**

a How many satellite channels are there?

....

b Do you have to cook your own breakfast?

....

c How much does a basic room cost per night?

....

d How many guests share a bathroom?

....

Focus on ... ab**C**def
adverbs used with adjectives

Ray uses all the words below when he describes his guesthouse. Look at the *audioscript* on page 95 and underline them.
really   very   fairly   quite   pretty

Do they come before or after an adjective? ....

How do they change the meaning of the adjective?

....

Did you know ...?

In Canada and the US, a *sink* is where you wash your hands and face. In the UK, Australia and New Zealand, a *sink* is where you wash dishes in the kitchen, and you wash your hands and face in a *basin*.

D Speaking – The guesthouse

Speaking strategy
Showing people things

1 **Look at what Ray says when he shows someone a room.**
Underline the expression that

> This is the lounge. It's got a widescreen TV ... and, as you can see, it's pretty comfortable.

a introduces the room.
b describes a particular feature.
c asks the listener to notice what the room is like.

Speak up!

2 Look at the pictures below. Use the words to help you describe them to another person.

Example: a
You say: This is my bedroom. It's got a really big bookcase. As you can see, it's pretty untidy.

a

really big bookcase   pretty untidy

d

20 Gb of memory   very light to carry around

b

a big screen   quite new

e

a zoom lens   fairly easy to carry in my pocket

c

a small engine   really easy to park

f

surround sound   almost like being at the movies

Class bonus

Describe objects that you own or have photos of to your classmates.

E X tra practice

Go to the Tourist Information Office in your city or town. Ask the information officer in English about accommodation there.

Can-do checklist

Tick what you can do.

	Can do	Need more practice
I can ask about different kinds of accommodation.		
I can understand important information about accommodation.		
I can describe rooms and objects.		

Unit 8
What can I do here?

Get ready to listen and speak

○ Look at the activities you can do in New Zealand. Tick ✓ the ones you have done.

go sailing ☐   visit a zoo ☐   go bungy jumping ☐

visit an aquarium ☐   go skydiving ☐   see dolphins and whales ☐

go to Useful language p. 80

A Listening – Different activities

1 🔵53 Calum has just arrived in Auckland so he visits the Tourist Information Centre and talks to Amy, the Tourist Information Officer. Listen to their conversation. Which activities from *Get ready* do they talk about?

2 🔵53 Listen again and complete the table. Remember to read the table first and think about what information is missing before you listen.

Activity	Details	Price ($)
See ᵃ _dolphins and whales_	ᵇ _____ am – 4 pm every day	ᶜ _____
Go ᵈ _____	ᵉ _____ metres high	ᶠ _____
Go ᵍ _____	ʰ _____ metres	250
Visit the aquarium	ⁱ _____ km from the centre of Auckland	ʲ _____

Learning tip

When you are listening to a CD, you get less information because you can't see the speakers. For example, in a Tourist Information Office, the officer will point to brochures and information inside them. This helps you to understand what he or she is saying.

B Speaking – Different activities

Speaking strategy
Showing you are interested

1 **Look at part of the conversation. Underline what Calum says to show he is interested in what the Tourist Information Officer is telling him.**

Officer: That is … $40.
Calum: Ah ha.
Officer: And they go every day.
Calum: Oh all right. And do you see dolphins every time?
Officer: Yes … well not absolutely guaranteed, not 100 per cent but they do … most of the time they will see dolphins or … it may be whales.
Calum: Oh wow.

2 **Look at the *audioscript* on page 93 and underline other words or expressions Calum uses to show he is interested. Write them here.**

--------------------------------------   --------------------------------------
--------------------------------------   --------------------------------------

Speak up!

3 🔊 **56** **Listen to Amy. Reply and show you are interested. Use a different expression each time. Remember to make your voice rise.**

Example: a
Amy: You can see dolphins and whales.
You say: Sounds good.

a Amy: You can see dolphins and whales.
b Amy: We have a tour every day.
   You say: ....
c Amy: It's a good idea to take your camera.
   You say: ....
d Amy: Usually it costs $140, but it's only $100 today.
   You say: ....
e Amy: You need to take your own lunch.
   You say: ....
f Amy: There are sometimes more than 50 dolphins.
   You say: ....

4 **What can visitors to your town or city do? Think of one activity and describe it in detail. Use the underlined expressions in Exercise 3 above to help you.**

C Listening – One activity

Calum goes back to the Tourist Information Office.

1 🔊 **157** **Listen to the conversation. What is Calum doing? Tick ✓ a, b or c.**

a getting more information about an activity ☐

b making a reservation for an activity ☐

c asking about a different activity ☐

2 🔊 **157** **Listen again and complete the form.**

Did you know ...?

You can do a lot of adventure (or adrenalin) sports like bungy jumping and skydiving in New Zealand. Other adventure sports include kite surfing, quad biking and river rafting.

Booking form

Activity:	ª skydiving
No of people:	b
Name:	c
Discount:	d YES / NO
Price:	e $
Day:	f
Date:	g

D Speaking – One activity

Speaking strategy
Talking about what you want to do

1 **Look at these sentences and answer the questions below.**

A I want to go skydiving.

B I'd like to go skydiving.

a Which sentence does Calum use?   A / B

b Which sentence is more polite?   A / B

c Look at sentence B. What does 'd mean?

....

Learning tip

Some sounds change when they are not stressed, for example:
can is pronounced /kən/ in *I can go this weekend.*
for is pronounced /fə/ in *Just for one person.*

Sound smart
Pronunciation of *would like to*

Contractions are used a lot in speaking, e.g. Calum says *I'd like* not *I would like.*

1 🔊 **158** Listen to the sentence and answer the questions.
   I'd like to go skydiving.
   Is *to* stressed? YES / NO
   Is *to* pronounced /tuː/ or /tə/? ....

2 🔊 **158** Listen again and repeat the sentence.

3 🔊 **159** Listen and repeat the other contractions with *would*.
   a he'd   b she'd   c it'd   d we'd   e they'd

4 Look at this sentence. *Would not* becomes *wouldn't*.
   I wouldn't like to go skydiving.

   🔊 **160** Listen and repeat.

Focus on ...
I'd like or I like

Look at what Calum is thinking as he is deciding what to do.

> **I like doing** new things and I've never been skydiving before so **I'd like to go** skydiving.

1 Which expression in **bold** describes something Calum wants to do?

Which expression in **bold** describes something Calum enjoys?

----

2 Which is correct? Tick ✓ a or b.
a I'd like going skydiving. ☐
b I'd like to go skydiving. ☐

3 Look at Calum's other ideas and choose the correct form.
a I love horse riding so I ~~like doing~~ / 'd like to do that tomorrow.
b I like going / 'd like to go shopping this afternoon because I want to buy presents for my friends.
c I 'm interested in history so I like going / 'd like to go to museums when I visit a new place.
d I like seeing / 'd like to see the dolphins while I'm in Auckland, but it's quite expensive so I don't think I can.

Speak up!

2 Talk about the activities in *Get ready*. Which would / wouldn't you like to do? Give reasons for your answers.

I'd like to …   I wouldn't like to …

Example:
You say: I'd like to go sailing because I love the sea but I wouldn't like to go bungy jumping because I don't like heights.

3 🔵 **61** Choose one activity from *Get ready*. Read the questions below. Think about your answers but do not write them. Then listen and answer.

Example: a
You hear: What did you decide to do?
You say: I'd like to go horseriding.

a What did you decide to do?
b What day do you want to go?
c For how many people?
d Can you give me your full name?
e How do you spell your surname?
f And I just need a contact telephone number as well.

Class bonus

A: You are the tourist information officer. Ask Student B questions to get the information you need to make a reservation.
B: You are a tourist and you would like to book an activity. Answer Student A's questions.
Then close your books and do the role play again.

E✗tra practice

Take a virtual tour of New Zealand at http://www.nz.com/new-zealand/tourism Then tell a friend in English what you would like to do if you visited New Zealand.

Can-do checklist

Tick what you can do.

	Can do	Need more practice
I can show I understand what someone is saying, and show that I am interested.	✓	✓
I can talk about what I want and would like to do.		
I can book an activity at a tourist information centre.		

Unit 9
When are you flying?

go to Useful language p. 80

Get ready to listen and speak

- Put the letters in the correct order to make a word about travelling. The first one has been done for you.

  1 pdtaer   d _epart_

  2 rriinatye   i_____

  3 ndtiatesnoi   d_____

  4 okibogn mrneub   b_____ n_____

  5 acclne   c_____

  6 rugaedp   u_____

- Now match the word to its definition.

  a a list of different places, times and dates for your travels _2_

  b when you pay extra money to change flight class ......

  c when you leave somewhere ......

  d when you tell somebody you do not want to do something that you organized earlier ......

  e an airline or travel agency gives you this to identify your reservation ......

  f the place that you arrive at ......

A Listening – The flight

1 🔊62 **Adam is on holiday in South Africa. In Johannesburg, he decides to change his travel plans so he speaks to Helen, a travel agent. Listen to their conversation. What does Adam ask to change? Tick ✓ a, b, c or d.**

a the airline ☐

b the travel date ☐

c the destination ☐

d the type of ticket ☐

2 🔊62 **Listen again and complete Helen's notes.**

Did you know ...?

When we say a flight number we say each individual number separately. We don't say the number as a total. So for SAA 235 we say: *SAA two, three, five,* not *SAA two hundred and thirty five.*

Destination:	ᵃ Cape Town			
Family name:	ᵇ		First name:	**Adam**
PREVIOUS TICKET				
Departure date:	ᶜ			
Flight number:	ᵈ			
Departure time:	ᵉ			
Ticket class:	ᶠ budget economy ☐ normal economy ☐			
NEW TICKET				
Departure date:	ᵍ			
Flight number:	**SAA 327**			
Departure time:	ʰ			
Ticket class:	ⁱ budget economy ☐ normal economy ☐			
Extra to pay:	ʲ [____] rand			

B Speaking – The flight

Speaking strategy
Asking polite questions

Adam asks Helen these two questions:

> Would it be possible to fly three days later?

> Is it possible to go in the morning?

He could also ask:

Can I fly three days later?
Could I go in the morning?

1 Put the questions below in order. 1 is the most polite and 3 is the most direct.

Would it be / Is it possible to fly tomorrow? ......
Can I fly tomorrow? ......
Could I fly tomorrow? ......

Sound smart
Stress of polite questions

1 ● **163** Listen to these two questions and underline the word stress.
  1 Would it be possible to fly three days later?
  2 Is it possible to go in the morning?

● **163** Listen again and repeat the two questions using the correct stress.

Did you know …?

London Heathrow is the world's busiest airport in terms of number of passengers (over 61 million in 2006).

Speak up!

2 Ask a travel agent questions about your flight using the words below.

Examples:

would / possible / fly three days later?   You say: Would it be possible to fly three days later?
is / possible / fly three days later?   You say: Is it possible to fly three days later?
could / fly three days later?   You say: Could I fly three days later?
can / fly three days later?   You say: Can I fly three days later?

a is / possible / travel a week later?
b would / possible / get a refund?
c could / change my hotel booking too?
d is / possible / leave the following day?

e can / buy travel insurance?
f would / possible / organize transport to the hotel?
g could / take an earlier flight?
h can / get a special meal on the flight?

C Listening – A change of plan

1 ● 164 Listen to Adam talking to Tom, a Tourist Information Officer in Cape Town. Look at the photos and match them to the statements below.

a Adam went to this place today. _____
b Adam cancels a trip to this place. _____
c Adam decides to go to this place. _____

2 ● 164 Listen again and correct the mistakes below.

a Adam went to Table Mountain ~~yesterday~~. today
b Adam cycled up Table Mountain.
c Adam hurt his back.
d Adam paid a deposit of 50 rand.
e The company needs 12 hours notice to cancel a booking.
f Adam will travel to Robben Island by helicopter.

Cape Point and Peninsula

Robben Island

Table Mountain

D Speaking – A change of plan

Speaking strategy
Giving reasons

1 In the conversation Adam talks about a situation and gives a reason for it. Look at these two sentences which have the same meaning:

    Reason   *Situation*
a I've hurt my leg so I can't do the cycling trip.

      Situation   *Reason*
b I can't do the cycling trip because I've hurt my leg.

What word joins the situation and reason in sentence a? _____

What word joins the situation and reason in sentence b? _____

2 <u>Underline</u> the situation and (circle) the reason in this sentence.

I've got really bad sunburn so I can't come to the beach.

Rewrite the sentence using *because.*

Speak up!

3 You are in Cape Town on holiday. Explain the situations below to the Tourist Information Officer. Think about the order and use the correct joining word, *because* or *so.*

Example: a
You say: I can't do the cycling trip because I'm really tired.
Example: b
You say: I'm really tired so I can't do the cycling trip.

  Situation   *Reason*
a can't do cycling trip ⟶ really tired

  Reason   *Situation*
b really tired ⟶ can't do cycling trip

  Reason   *Situation*
c afraid of flying ⟶ can't travel by plane

  Situation   *Reason*
d can't go on the boat trip ⟶ get seasick very easily

  Reason   *Situation*
e special ticket ⟶ can't change my flight

  Reason   *Situation*
f haven't got enough money ⟶ can't come to the restaurant with you

  Situation   *Reason*
g can't go hiking ⟶ haven't got the right shoes

  Reason   *Situation*
h haven't got a driver's licence ⟶ can't hire a car

Focus on ...
So

In *Speak up!* you used *so* to explain a situation.

I've hurt my leg so I can't do the cycling trip.

Look at examples 1 to 3 which use *so* and match them with the explanations in a to c below.

1 When I passed the exam I was *so* happy.
2 A: Can you still come to my party?
   B: I hope *so*.
3 *So* where are you going on holiday this year?

a *So* is used to avoid repeating language. It can also be used in this way with verbs like: *think*, *believe*, *be afraid*.
b *So* is used to introduce a new topic into a conversation.
c *So* is used as an adverb to make the meaning of an adjective stronger.

4 🔊 65 **Use the conversation map below to help you have a conversation with Tom, the Tourist Information Officer.**

Tom

Hello. Can I help you?

That's a pity. Well, you could hire a car for a day.

Oh dear. Well, you could do a day bus trip.

You

Explain the situation and give a reason.

Say you don't want to and say why it's not possible.

Agree that this is a good idea.

Class bonus

Work in pairs and role play changing an activity or a flight. Remember to say why you want to change it.

E X tra practice

Most travel agents speak English so next time you book a holiday, ask your travel agent if you can make the booking in English.

Learning tip

To help you remember new words, it is useful to use mind maps. Look at this example which uses words from this unit.

Copy this mind map into your vocabulary book and add some more words from the unit.

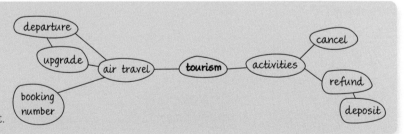

Can-do checklist

Tick what you can do.

	Can do	Need more practice
I can understand information about travel and tourism.	✓	✓
I can ask polite questions.		
I can give reasons for situations.		

Unit 10
The weather is changing

go to Useful language p. 80

Get ready to listen and speak

- Match the picture to the word.
  1 snow ..a..
  2 flood ......
  3 drought ......
  4 cyclone ......
  5 storm ......
  6 heat wave ......

- Are any of these weather conditions a problem in your country?

A Listening – A news story

1 🎧 166 Listen to the beginning of a radio programme about global warming. Tick ✓ the weather conditions in *Get ready* that are mentioned.

2 🎧 166 Listen again and complete these notes.

Global Warming

Problems

<u>In Britain</u>
Hot weather is causing problems with:
- 🌍 ᵃ _work_
- 🌍 sleep
- 🌍 ᵇ _____ – 100 people have ᶜ _____
Temperatures above 30ºC are becoming more ᵈ _____

<u>Around the world</u>
- 🌍 Europe is having the hottest summer in ᵉ _____ years
- 🌍 In Antarctica, the ice is melting.
- 🌍 Temperatures will rise by 5ºC in the next ᶠ _____ years.
- 🌍 ᵍ _____ in India.
- 🌍 Fires in the United States
- 🌍 More ʰ _____ in the South Pacific.

Reasons

<u>Experts say:</u>
- 🌍 Temperatures are rising because there is too much ⁱ _____
- 🌍 It is part of a natural cycle and we are not causing it.

Learning tip

Try to understand the words that are strongly stressed because these are often the most important words.

Did you know …?

In the US, temperature is measured in degrees Fahrenheit (ºF). In the UK, Australia, Canada and New Zealand, temperature is measured in degrees Celsius or Centigrade (ºC). Water boils at 212ºF and 100ºC.

B Speaking – A news story

Speaking strategy
Talking about change

1 Look at the sentences from the text. To talk about changes, we often use *get* or *become* and a comparative adjective like *warmer* or *more common*.

> Temperatures above 30° **are becoming more common**.

> The weather **is getting warmer**.

In the sentences above, what tense are *get* and *become* in? ....

You can also use *more*, *less* and *fewer* with nouns to describe change.

There were **more** cyclones this year than last year.
There was **less** snow this year.
There are **fewer** forests.

2 Which of these words do you use *fewer* with? Which do you use *less* with? Write them in the correct column.

cars	ice	pollution	floods	rain	energy	aeroplanes	fires

fewer	less
cars	

Note: We use *less* with uncountable words and *fewer* with countable words, but sometimes in spoken English you will hear *less* used with all nouns.

Sound smart
Stressing important information

1 🔊 **67** Listen to some questions asked in the text. In each question, the most important information is stressed. Which word has the strongest stress? Underline one word in each sentence.
   a So what's causing all this?
   b Are these changes due to global warming?
   c Are we causing these problems?

2 Here are some other sentences from the text. For each sentence underline the words which you think have the strongest stress.
   a It's <u>difficult</u> to <u>work.</u>
   b It's difficult to sleep.
   c It's causing health problems.
   d In Antarctica, the ice is melting.
   e The earth is getting hotter.
   f We've heard about the floods in India.

3 🔊 **68** Listen and check your answers.

4 Listen again and practise saying the sentences with the correct stress.

Speak up!

3 Talk about the changes in the summer and winter in your country over the last ten years.

   Example: a
   You say: Summer is getting hotter or Winter is getting colder.
   a get hotter/colder
   b get longer/shorter
   c get colder/warmer
   d start earlier/later
   e there / more/less rain
   f there / more/fewer storms

4 Describe any other changes in the weather in your country recently.

5 Choose three of the topics below and make sentences to describe the situation in your country. Use *more / less / fewer* or *get / become + -er.*

   Example:
   You say: There are more hospitals now.
           Mobile phones are getting smaller.

unemployment	hospitals	petrol	education
public transport	food	air travel	mobile phones
free time			

C Listening – Talking about the news

1 You are going to hear three people talking about global warming. Write four words about global warming you think you will hear.

....

2 🔊 69 Listen and tick ✓ any words you hear that you wrote in Exercise 1.

Learning tip

If you know the topic of a conversation, it is a good idea to think about what you know about that topic before you listen. This makes it easier to understand the conversation.

3 🔊 69 Listen again. Tick ✓ the correct speaker(s) for each statement.

	Speaker 1	Speaker 2	Speaker 3
a Who doesn't think global warming is causing all our weather problems?			
b Who (2 people) talks about how we can stop global warming?			
c Who talks about changes in the Arctic?			
d Who (2 people) talks about problems with the weather?			

4 🔊 69 Listen again and answer these questions.

a Speaker 1:
   What is one problem caused by global warming?

   ----

b Speakers 2 and 3:
   What are three things people could do to reduce pollution?

D Speaking – Talking about the news

Speaking strategy
Giving opinions

a I'm not convinced that all our weather problems are because of global warming.

b I'm not an expert but … I think we have created a lot of pollution.

c It seems to me that the weather's changing.

d I think that's because of global warming.

e In my opinion, we can do something about it.

f I guess that will make a difference.

1 Underline the words the speakers use to give their opinions.

Which expression means the speaker doesn't believe something?

Which expression means the speaker doesn't have any special knowledge about the subject?

Speak up!

2 🔊 **70 What do you think about global warming? Listen to the questions below and give your opinion. Try to use all the expressions in *Speaking strategy*.**

Example: a
You say: I'm not an expert but I think it's getting hotter.

a Is the weather getting hotter?
b Is global warming a big problem?
c How are people making global warming worse?
d What can we do to stop global warming?
e Should individual people or governments clean up the environment?

Learning tip

When you give your opinion, it is important to explain your ideas. This helps keep the conversation going and makes it more interesting for the listener.

3 **What is your opinion on the following statements? Explain your ideas.**

Example: a
You say: I'm not convinced children have an easier life than adults, because
        they have to learn a lot of new things and adults always tell them what
        to do.

a Children have an easier life than adults.
b English is easy to learn.
c Smoking should be illegal.
d Aeroplane tickets are too cheap.
e Mobile phones should be banned in public places (e.g. trains, shops etc.).
f Money is the most important thing in a job.

Class bonus

In groups, talk about a story in the news and discuss your opinions of it. It could be about sport, entertainment, local or international news.

E X tra practice

Listen to the news in English on the TV, radio or online. Some useful websites are
http://www.voanews.com/specialenglish
http://www.bbc.co.uk/worldservice/learningenglish/newsenglish/index.shtml
http://edition.cnn.com/services/podcasting
Use Appendix 4 'Listening to the news' on page 83 to help you.

Can-do checklist

Tick what you can do.

	Can do	Need more practice
I can understand a news story.		
I can talk about change.		
I can give my opinion.		

Review 1
Units 1–10

Section 1

For each question tick ✓ a, b or c.

1 When you listen to a text for the first time you should
  a try to understand everything. ☐
  b try to understand the general idea. ☐
  c stop when you don't understand something. ☐

2 To check information you can
  a repeat everything the speaker said. ☐
  b wait and hope the speaker will say it again. ☐
  c repeat part of what the speaker said and wait for ☐
    them to finish the sentence.

3 Which expression is **not** a way of making a suggestion?
  a We could go to the movies. ☐
  b We should go to the movies. ☐
  c What about going to the movies? ☐

4 Which expression talks about the ingredients of a meal?
  a It's like spaghetti. ☐
  b It's made with peppers and lamb. ☐
  c It's got a strong flavour. ☐

5 In a conversation you should
  a only ask questions. ☐
  b only answer questions. ☐
  c ask and answer questions. ☐

6 What is the best way to describe something?
  a give a general description. ☐
  b give a general description and then give more ☐
    detail.
  c give a detailed description and then a general ☐
    description.

7 If you are feeling nervous about speaking English in real life situations, e.g. at the bank or chemist, what should you do?
  a Practise what you want to say before you go. ☐
  b Take your dictionary and look up new words ☐
    when you are there.
  c Take a friend with you so they can translate for ☐
    you.

8 Which of these expressions is making a general enquiry?
  a I'm not keen on sharing a bedroom. ☐
  b I'm looking for somewhere to stay. ☐
  c That sounds interesting. ☐

9 Which expression does **not** describe what a hotel room looks like?
  a It's fairly big. ☐
  b It's clean and comfortable. ☐
  c It costs £40 a night. ☐

10 Which expression is the most polite?
  a I want to go to the cinema. ☐
  b I'd like to go to the cinema. ☐
  c Let's go to the cinema. ☐

11 Which request is the most polite?
  a Would it be possible to travel a day later? ☐
  b Can I travel a day later? ☐
  c How about travelling a day later? ☐

12 Which expression does **not** talk about a change in something?
  a The traffic is getting worse. ☐
  b There is more traffic now. ☐
  c The traffic is noisy. ☐

13 Which expression does **not** describe an opinion?
  a I guess we should try to make the environment ☐
    cleaner.
  b I said we need to make the environment cleaner. ☐
  c It seems to me we need to make the ☐
    environment cleaner.

Section 2

Answer these questions.

14 What are some good topics to talk about when you are starting a conversation with someone you don't know very well?

----

15 Your shower doesn't work. Telephone your landlord. Tell him and offer a solution.

----

16 When you read questions in a listening task, what is it a good idea to think about?

----

17 Make a suggestion using the words below
Shall / go / Thai restaurant

----

18 Tell someone what you ate using the words below.
Italian restaurant / dessert / tiramisu / delicious / coffee and cream

----

----

19 Write a sentence to describe the word *apple*. Use *kind of.*

----

20 Rewrite this sentence: *I forgot my ticket so I can't travel.* Use *because.*

----

21 Rewrite this sentence: *I can't go swimming because I didn't bring my swimming costume.* Use *so.*

Section 3

🔊 71 Listen and answer these questions.

22 Listen and tick ✓ the best reply to the invitation.
I'm having a party on Friday. Do you want to come?
a No. ☐
b That sounds lovely but I'm afraid I have to work on Friday. ☐
c I have to work on Friday. ☐

23 Listen and <u>underline</u> the stressed words in this question.
Can I buy a discount card from all stations or only from some stations?

24 Listen and tick ✓ the best reply to this sentence.
Did you see the match last night?
a Yes, I did see the match last night. ☐
b Yes, I did. ☐
c Yes, I didn't see it. ☐

25 Listen and give the person some advice.
I have a headache.

26 Listen and give the person some advice.
I have a sore throat.

27 Listen and show you are interested.
You can go kayaking.

28 Listen and show you are interested.
It costs $20.

29 Listen and (circle) the unstressed word.
I'd like to go surfing.

30 Listen and tick ✓ the sentence which shows the correct stress.
a Pollution <u>is</u> getting worse
b <u>Pollution</u> is getting worse
c Pollution is <u>getting</u> worse

Unit 11
I have our schedule

○ What is your favourite kind of coffee? Tick ✓ the box.
espresso ☐   cappuccino ☐   filter ☐   instant ☐   none ☐

○ What do you know about coffee? Read the sentences and decide if they are true (T) or false (F).
Coffee is grown on a tree. ......
The word 'coffee' comes from the French word 'café'. ......
The country that produces the most coffee is Brazil. ......

go to Useful language p. 80

A Listening – Plans for the day

Declan is a businessman from Ireland. He goes on a trip to São Paulo, Brazil, to visit the company 'Café Perfeito do Brasil'. He is interested in importing coffee.

1 🔊② **Listen to the conversation and match the job title to the people below.**

a   Lilian Oliveira
b   Teresa Silva
c   Paulo Souza
d   Fernando Pinto
e   Victor Gomez

2 Declan will do the activities below during his visit. The activities are in the wrong order. Can you remember the correct order? Write the number by the activity. The first one has been done for you.

Order	Activity	What time?
....	Have lunch with the CEO.	....
....	Meet the Marketing Manager.	....
....	Visit the factory.	....
1	Talk to the Sales Manager.	10 am
....	Relax in the hotel before dinner.	....
....	Visit a coffee plantation by helicopter.	....
....	Taste different coffee.	....

3 🔊② **Listen again and check your answers. Write the times Declan will do each activity in the 'What time?' column.**

B Speaking – Plans for the day

Speaking strategy
Talking about schedules

Lilian uses the expressions below to explain the schedule to Declan.

> First of all, you'll meet my colleague.

> Then she's going to introduce you to Paulo Souza.

> After that you're having lunch at 12.30 with Fernando.

> Later on you'll be able to visit the factory.

1 The expressions above all talk about future time. <u>Underline</u> the verb(s) in each sentence that shows future time. The first one has been done for you.

Speak up!

2 Lilian visits the company you work for. She asks you about her schedule. Listen and answer her questions using the notes below to help you.

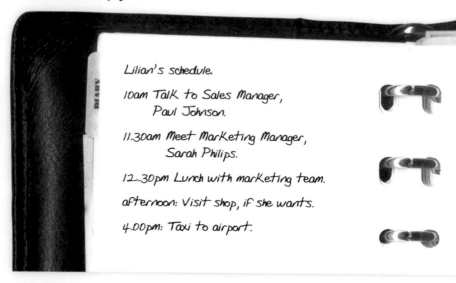

Lilian's schedule.

10am Talk to Sales Manager, Paul Johnson.

11.30am Meet Marketing Manager, Sarah Philips.

12.30pm Lunch with marketing team.

afternoon: Visit shop, if she wants.

4.00pm: Taxi to airport.

3 Listen to someone describing Lilian's schedule.

> This is your schedule for the day. First, you're going to talk to the Sales Manager, Paul Johnson, at ten o'clock this morning. Then at half past eleven you're meeting the Marketing Manager, Sarah Philips. After that, you'll have lunch with the marketing team at half past twelve. This afternoon you'll be able to visit our shop, if you want. I've booked a taxi to the airport at four o'clock this afternoon.

4 Cover the example answer in Exercise 3 and use the notes in Exercise 2 to say something similar. Don't worry if what you say is not exactly the same as the example.

5 Now tell another visitor, Peter Richards, about his schedule. Use the expressions from *Speaking strategy*.

Peter Richards' schedule.

2pm Meet Office Manager, Debbie Fulton.

2.30pm Talk to office staff, if he wants.

3pm Have afternoon tea with Debbie & Customer Services Manager, Sam Harris.

3.30pm Meet Company Director, Suzanne Allen.

Tonight: Hotel accommodation booked at The Regent Hotel.

Learning tip

Sometimes it's useful to read an example answer aloud, but don't memorize it. Learning to speak from notes rather than reading aloud is difficult, but it helps you get better at speaking freely.

Did you know …?

In the UK, Ireland, Australia, New Zealand and South Africa, a *schedule* is a plan of what people will do at different times. In the US a *schedule* is also a timetable for buses and trains.

C Listening – Future plans

1 🔘5 After his visit, Declan took a taxi to the airport. Listen to his conversation with the taxi driver, Gustavo. Which summary of their conversation is correct? Tick ✓ a or b.

a Declan wants to buy Brazilian coffee for his cafés in Ireland. He wants good quality coffee. ☐

b Declan wants to buy Brazilian coffee to sell in his food shops in Ireland. He wants coffee at a good price. ☐

2 🔘5 Listen again and answer the questions about Declan.

a How many cafés does he own in Cork?

----

b What is his opinion of his visit to 'Café Perfeito do Brasil'?

----

c What does he think of the coffee in the large café chains?

----

d What does he want to do in the future?

----

e What surprised Declan about São Paulo?

----

3 🔘6 Listen to Declan talk about two of his future plans. Put one word in each space to complete the sentences.

a I _____ _____ _____
coffee that is _____ _____ some of
_____ _____ chains.

b I'd _____ _____ expand
_____ _____ up _____
cafés.

Did you know ...?

Declan says *That's grand.*
In Ireland, people say *grand* to mean 'good' or 'great'.

D Speaking – Future plans

Speaking strategy
Talking about future plans

1 Declan uses the expressions in **bold** to talk
about future plans.

> **I plan to** make coffee that is better.

> **I'd like to** expand.

Other expressions you can use are:

> **I hope to** increase business.

> **I intend to** open a new store.

> **I want to** buy Brazilian coffee.

Which expression is strongest?

Focus on ...
verbs followed by *to*

Notice how all the verbs in *Speaking strategy*
are followed by *to* and another verb.

1 Look at the verbs below. Only five of them can be
followed by *to* + verb. Circle them.

choose	think	hear	offer
try	guess	expect	promise
understand	say		

2 Which pattern follows the other five verbs? Tick ✓ a or b.
   a verb + *-ing* ☐
   b *that* + subject + verb ☐

Speak up!

2 **You own a business. Make sentences
about your future business plans using the
expressions below.**

Example: a
You say: I plan to open a new shop.

a plan / open a new shop
b like / hire an assistant
c plan / sell more products online
d hope / employ more staff
e want/ close one of our factories
f like / increase our profits
g intend/ export more products
h plan / do more marketing abroad

3 **Talk about your own hopes and plans for the
future. You can talk about the things below.**

– your studies or work
– your family life
– your sports and hobbies

E✗tra practice

You can get more listening practice about business at the
BBC Learning English website:
http://www.bbc.co.uk/worldservice/learningenglish/
business/

Class bonus

Talk in groups about your schedule for the day or week.
Who has the busiest week?

Can-do checklist

Tick what you can do.

	Can do	Need more practice
I can understand people's names and roles.		
I can explain and understand schedules.		
I can talk about and understand future plans.		

Unit 12
You did really well

Get ready to listen and speak

- Match the job to a task.

Jobs	Tasks
1 waitress	a answers telephone calls
2 manager	b brings food to people
3 mechanic	c runs a business
4 call centre worker	d repairs cars

go to Useful language p. 80

A Listening – Getting ready

Francesca is an Italian student studying in Bristol. She works part-time as a waitress. It is her first day at work.

Did you know ...?

In the US more than two million people work as waiters or waitresses. It is one of the most popular jobs in the US. Nursing and teaching are also popular.

1 🔊17 Carrie is Francesca's boss. Listen to them discuss Francesca's tasks for the evening. Tick ✓ what Francesca has done.

2 🔊17 Listen again. What two things will Carrie check?

a ....
b ....

✔ a Fill the sugar bowls on the tables.
b Put knives and forks on the tables.
c Put napkins on the tables.
d Put water jugs in the refrigerator to cool.
e Put menus on the tables.
f Put salt and pepper on every table.
g Put flowers on the tables.
h Put the glasses out on the tables.
i Light the candles.
j Cut the bread.

B Speaking – Getting ready

Speaking strategy
Talking about completed tasks with *yet* and *already*

1 Francesca talks about what she has and hasn't done:

> I've **already** filled the sugar bowls.

> I haven't put the menus on the tables **yet**.

Carrie asks Francesca:

> Have you put those out **yet**?

Look at what Carrie and Francesca said and tick the correct columns.

We use:	in positive sentences	in negative sentences	in questions
already			
yet			

Which word comes at the end of a sentence? (Circle) it.

yet / already

> **Learning tip**
>
> When learning useful expressions, it's a good idea to look for patterns or things in common, for example, when you want to talk about completed actions and the time isn't important, we use the pattern:
> *I + have + verb*
> *e.g. I've filled or I've put …*
>
> Looking for patterns in language is a useful way of helping you to remember expressions.

Speak up!

2 You are working in a restaurant. Say what you have already done and what you have not done yet. Use *I have* or *I haven't* plus the correct form of the verb.

Example: a
You say: I've already filled the water jugs.
Example: b
You say: I haven't filled the water jugs yet.

a   fill / water jugs / (*already*)
b   fill / water jugs / (*yet*)
c   arrange / flowers / (*already*)
d   check / reservations list / (*yet*)
e   talk / chef / menu / (*already*)
f   put / knives and forks / tables / (*already*)
g   turn on /music / (*yet*)
h   write / menu / board / (*yet*)
i   cut / bread / (*already*)
j   light / candles / (*yet*)

3 You are the manager of a clothes shop. Ask if the tasks below have been done.

Example: a
You say: Have you tidied the clothes yet?

a   tidy / clothes
b   check / till
c   turn on / computer
d   sweep / floor
e   unlock / door

> **Class bonus**
>
> Ask other students whether they have done the things below today:
> *meet friends / study / have dinner / go online*
> Use *yet* and *already* when you ask and answer the questions.

C Listening – A busy evening

Learning tip

When you listen to people talking, try to listen to how they sound as well as what they say. The tone of their voice can give you useful information about the person's attitude, for example, whether they are feeling positive or negative, or happy or sad.

1 🔘**8** **Carrie and Francesca talk again later. Listen and tick ✓ a or b.**

1 When do they talk?
  a half-way through serving meals ☐
  b at the end of the evening ☐
2 How does Carrie feel about Francesca's work?
  a mostly positive ☐
  b mostly negative ☐
3 How much money did Francesca make in tips?
  a £15 ☐
  b £35 ☐

2 🔘**8** **Carrie made notes on Francesca's work during the evening. Listen again and complete them. Write one word in each gap.**

> Francesca
>
> Overall: went ᵃ _____well_____
>
> good points:
> • is ᵇf_____ and n_____ with customers
> ways to improve:
> • ᶜc_____ p_____ as soon as possible.
> • keep the ᵈw_____ g_____ filled
>
> gets good ᵉt_____

Did you know …?

In the UK and Ireland, it is usual to tip about 10% in a restaurant. In the US, waiters expect a tip of 15% to 20% and in South Africa they expect 10% to 15%. In Australia and New Zealand, waiters don't expect a tip, but it is always appreciated if you leave one.

D Speaking – A busy evening

Speaking strategy
Giving feedback

1 **Look at the feedback Carrie gives Francesca on her work. Tick ✓ the positive feedback. Put a cross ✗ by the negative feedback.**

   a You did really well. ✓
   b Can you just make sure you clear the plates as soon as possible? ☐
   c It'd be really good if you could just try to keep the water glasses filled. ☐
   d That's really good for your first night. ☐
   e There are just a few little things … ☐
   f I think you're a natural. ☐

2 **Look at the negative feedback. Every sentence contains *just*. Why do you think Carrie says this?**

Speak up!

3 🔊 **10 You work in a restaurant. Give Sergei, a new waiter, feedback after his first shift.**

   Look at this conversation and try to make the negative feedback softer by using *can you*, *could you* and *just*. Then listen and speak to Sergei.

   You: You did well tonight. There are a few things.
   Sergei: Oh right.
   You: Try to get the meals out as soon as possible.
   Sergei: Yes sure.
   You: And make sure you change the napkins after each course.
   Sergei: Sure. Anything else?
   You: Yes, clear the plates quickly.
   Sergei: OK.

Sound smart
Linking between words

🔊 **9** Look at these expressions from b and e in *Speaking strategy*, and listen to them.

… the plates as soon as possible.

There are just a few …

When the last sound of a word is a consonant sound and the first sound of the next word is a vowel, they are often linked together (ʊ).

Can you find another example of this kind of linking in expressions a–f?

----

4 **Use the words below to give negative and positive feedback. Use the expressions in *Speaking strategy* to help you. Remember to make the negative feedback softer.**

   a make sure / smile / customers / arrive
   b think / very good waiter
   c check / give customers / correct glasses
   d excellent / first night
   e good if / bring / bill more quickly

Class bonus

When did you last go to a restaurant? How was the service? Was the waiter / waitress friendly and helpful? Did you have to wait long for your food? Did you leave a tip? Talk about these questions in small groups. Who had the best experience? Who had the worst?

E ✗ tra practice

Plan an English-speaking evening. Invite some friends who speak English. Cook together and speak English during the preparation time as well as when you are eating.

Can-do checklist

Tick what you can do.

	Can do	Need more practice
I can understand conversations about tasks in the workplace.		
I can talk about whether tasks are completed or not.		
I can give and understand feedback.		

Unit 13
I've organized the trainer

○ Use the pictures below to complete the crossword. The first letter of each word is given.

Across
5   6   9

Down
1   2   3

4   7   8

○ Tick ✓ the things you have used this week.

go to Useful language p. 81

A Listening – Organizing the training

Brad is a team leader at the Vulcan Power Company in Sydney. Raman works in Brad's team.

1 🔊11 Brad leaves Raman a voice mail message about organizing a training session. Listen to the message and tick ✓ the things in *Get ready* which he mentions.

2 🔊11 Raman made some notes but he got a few things wrong. Listen again and correct his notes. There is one mistake in every sentence.

a Brad can't come because he is ill. his son
b The training session is today.

  I need to:
c book the room.
d talk to trainer about the projector.
e arrange lunch for 15 people.
f give everyone a folder and a pen.
g get several flip charts.

Did you know …?

In this unit, there are examples of Australian English. Brad says *crook* and *this arvo. Crook* means 'sick' or 'unwell' and *this arvo* means 'this afternoon'. In *Listening C* you will hear someone say *g'day* and *beaut. G'day* is short for good day and means 'hello' and *beaut* is short for 'beautiful' and means 'great' or 'fantastic'.

B Speaking – Organizing the training

Speaking strategy
Asking people to do things

1 Look at how Brad asks Raman to do things.

> **I need you to** organize the projector.

> **You'll need to** sort out lunch.

Is Brad polite or direct when he asks Raman to do things? ....

Could Raman ask Brad to do things using *I need you to* and *You'll need to*?

YES / NO

2 Look at the expressions below. Tick ✓ the ones Raman could use to ask Brad to do things.

Could you … ☐
I want you to … ☐
Would you be able to … ☐
Do you think you could … ☐
Make sure you … ☐

Speak up!

3 You are organizing a training session. Ask Mariusz, a team member, to help you. Use the polite expressions from *Speaking strategy* to ask Mariusz to organize the things below.

Example: a
You say: Could you order a taxi?

a order / taxi
b buy / pens
c order / flowers
d send / email
e book / hotel room
f organize / morning tea
g get / laptop

Learning tip

Thing means the same as 'object' in the example in *Focus on*. For materials, liquids or groups of objects we use the word *stuff*, e.g. *some stuff for cleaning the whiteboard*.

Focus on …
when you don't know the right word

Look at how Brad explains a word he can't remember.

> and one of those … what do you call them? … you know, one of those really big things, like a pad of paper for writing up notes … flip charts.

a What expression does Brad use to show he is not sure of a word? ....
b What word means 'object'? ....
c Underline the words which say what we do with a flip chart.
d What word compares the flip chart to a similar object?
....

4 Explain the objects in the pictures below. Use the expressions from *Focus on* to help you.

Example: a
You say: a thing like a big camera for showing pictures and photos on a big screen

a

b

e

c
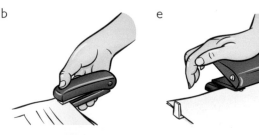

f

d

g

C Listening – Choosing lunch

1 🎧12 Raman talks to Alison, the receptionist at the Vulcan Power Company, about the training session. Listen to their conversation. What does Raman do? Tick ✓ a, b or c.

a give instructions ☐
b explain a decision ☐
c ask for help making a choice ☐

2 🎧12 Listen again and complete the information in the table.

	The Tasman Café	The Lunch Box
Delivery charge	$10	$20
Where café is		
	--------------------------------	--------------------------------
Type of food	gourmet sandwiches	normal sandwiches

Total price	$ --------------------------------	$ --------------------------------

D Speaking – Choosing lunch

Speaking strategy
Comparing things

1 **Look at how Raman and Alison compare the two cafés and underline the language that they use to make comparisons. The first one has been done for you.**

Alison: I mean, the food from The Tasman Café is probably nicer.

Raman: Well, The Tasman Café has gourmet sandwiches, not just ordinary sandwiches.

So, you know, the food will probably taste better from The Tasman Café.

You get much more variety.

But The Lunch Box is cheaper.

Their delivery charge is more expensive.

Sound smart
Sentence stress when comparing things

1 🎧13 Listen to the sentence below. Underline the two words which have the strongest stress.

The Tasman Café has gourmet sandwiches, not just ordinary sandwiches.

2 🎧14 Listen and repeat the sentences. Use the words below to help you.
a vegetarian sushi / ordinary sushi
b hot savouries / cold savouries
c chocolate cake / orange cake
d fresh coffee / instant coffee

Speak up!

2 🔊**15** **Raman is organizing lunch for a conference. He asks you for your opinion about the food he should order. Read the questions below and listen.**

Raman: Hi there. I'm ordering food for the conference. Can I ask you some questions?
You: Yes, of course.
Raman: Do you prefer hot or cold food?
You: cold food / easy
Raman: OK, and what about drinks – do you prefer hot or cold?
You: hot drinks / good
Raman: I'm trying to decide between a buffet or a sit-down meal. What do you think?
You: buffet / convenient
Raman: And should I order fruit or cake for dessert?
You: fruit / healthy

3 🔊**16** **Now listen and answer Raman's questions.**

4 **Think of two things you know well and you can compare with each other, e.g. two cars or two cities or two restaurants. Talk about the differences between these two things. Use *Speaking strategy* to help you.**

Class bonus

You are at the training lunch. Go around the class and ask questions about food and drink you prefer.

E✗tra practice

To hear more examples of Australian English, go to the ABC (Australian Broadcasting Corporation) website and listen to a radio stream http://www.abc.net.au

Can-do checklist

Tick what you can do.

	Can do	Need more practice
I can understand instructions in a voice mail message.		
I can ask people at work to do things.		
I can compare two things.		

Unit 14
You need a budget

Get ready to listen and speak

○ Tick ✓ the things you think a financial advisor would recommend.

save money ☐	use credit cards ☐
keep to a budget ☐	borrow money ☐

earn a good salary ☐   pay tax on time ☐
plan for retirement ☐   invest money ☐

go to Useful language p. 81

A Listening – Managing money 1

Managing Money

Important tips:

1 Watch how much you ᵃ........spend........
   - don't overspend, e.g. if you earn $2000, don't spend $2500.
   - cut back on ᵇ........................ things.

2 Check how much you ᶜ........................
   - before you accept a job, compare your ᵈ........................ with similar jobs in other companies.
   - make sure you get paid ᵉ........................

3 Have a ᶠ........................ i.e. a simple financial plan
   - ᵍ........................ it. Don't forget it.

1 🔘17 **Paul Dugan is a financial advisor. He is giving a seminar to students in their last year of university. Listen to the first part of the seminar and tick ✓ the things in *Get ready* that he talks about.**

2 **Sara went to Paul's seminar and took notes, but she missed some information. Read her notes and complete any information you can remember.**

3 🔘17 **Listen again and complete Sara's notes.**

Did you know ...?

It's a good idea to use *e.g.* and *i.e.* when you take notes to save time (*e.g.* means *for example* and *i.e.* means *that is*).

B Speaking – Managing money 1

Speaking strategy
Organizing a talk

1 Look at how Paul organizes the different parts of his seminar.

> **I'm going to talk to you about** how to manage money.

> **The first point is about** how much you spend.

> **The next point is about** how much you earn.

> **Another important point is** that you need a budget.

Which expression in bold does Paul use to introduce the topic?

Can *The next point is* and *Another point is* be used at the beginning of the talk?

YES / NO

2 Here are the expressions Paul uses in the second part of the seminar. Do you think he uses A or B first?

A | **My final tip** for managing your money is …

B | **My fourth point is** …

3 Look at the expressions above. Should you use them when you are talking to your friends about everyday topics? Why / Why not?

Speak up!

Learning tip

When you give a talk or a seminar, give examples to explain what you mean. This makes it easier for the listener to understand your opinion. Paul says *It's really important that you don't overspend. For example, if you earn $2000 a month, don't spend $2500.*

4 Choose a topic from the box below or choose one of your own and plan a mini seminar. Think about what you will say and how you will organize your talk. Use the expressions in *Speaking strategy* and make notes to help you. Start like this:

Good morning / afternoon / evening. Today I'm going to talk to you about …

> Why sport is important
> A great place for a holiday
> The advantages of living in a city
> The perfect job

5 Practise saying your mini seminar. Then say it again and record yourself. Listen to the recording and answer the questions below.

Did you introduce your topic clearly? YES / NO
Did you organize your ideas clearly? YES / NO
Did you use the expressions in *Speaking strategy*? YES / NO
Did you give examples to explain your points? YES / NO

C Listening – Managing money 2

1 🔘 **18 Now listen to the second part of Paul's seminar. Does Paul give the following advice?**

a You should never borrow money.
YES / NO

b You should use credit cards carefully.
YES / NO

c As you start to earn more, you can save less.
YES / NO

2 🔘 **18 Listen again and complete Sara's notes below.**

4 Manage your debt
Think about what you borrow money for:
. borrow to buy assets e.g. ᵃ____a house____ or education
. don't borrow money for things which aren't essential e.g.
ᵇ
_____ _____ _____

It's important to know how much you spend on your ᶜ_____ :
. pay the whole bill every ᵈ_____
. if you pay small amounts, you also pay ᵉ_____ so you pay more for something.

5 Plan your savings
. save ᶠ_____ per cent of your salary.
. try to increase how much you save every ᵍ_____ .

D Speaking – Managing money 2

Speaking strategy
Asking follow-up questions

1 After a presentation, you can ask two types of questions.

Type A: to ask for more detail about something talked about in the seminar.
Type B: to ask about something related to the topic of the seminar.

Some students asked Paul these questions. Are they type A or B?

a I'd like to ask when you should talk to your employer about how much you earn. _____

b I'm interested in knowing what kind of bank account you should have. _____

c You talked about saving. What happens if you can't save ten per cent of your salary? _____

d Do you think it's safe to use the internet for banking?
_____

Focus on ...
how to ask follow-up questions

Look at the questions in *Speaking strategy*.
These expressions are used to make the questions less direct.
I'd like to ask …
I'm interested in knowing …
You talked about saving.
Do you think …

1 Which expression summarizes the topic before asking the question?
_____

2 Choose the correct form of each question.
a I'd like to ask how I can get a job that pays a lot of money.
I'd like to ask how can I get a job that pays a lot of money.
b I'm interested in knowing where I get more information from.
I'm interested in knowing where do I get more information from.

3 Use the expressions above to make these questions less direct.
a How much is a good salary?
b How do I get a financial advisor?
c What should I invest in?
d Is it a good idea to have more than one bank account?

Speak up!

2 Match each seminar topic to a suitable question.

Seminar topics	Questions
1 The importance of saving money ___b___	a What's the best way to practise speaking?
2 Playing a musical instrument _____	b How can I save for my retirement?
3 Learning English on your own _____	c How much exercise should I do each week?
4 The problem of global warming _____	d Do we use mobile phones too much?
5 Keeping healthy _____	e What can we do to help clean up the environment?
6 Technology makes life easier _____	f Which is the easiest one to learn?

3 Use the expressions in *Focus on* to make the questions in Exercise 2 less direct.

Example: a
You say: I'm interested in knowing the best way to practise speaking.

4 Ask Paul Dugan three questions about his seminar. You can listen to the seminar again and / or read the audioscript on page 98.

Learning tip

It's often a good idea to record new vocabulary in groups because it makes them easier to remember. For example, in this unit there are a lot of words about money.

verbs + money	nouns
earn	tax
spend	budget
save	debt
invest	savings
borrow	interest

Class bonus

In groups give a short presentation on one of the seminar topics in *Speak up!* or choose one of your own and ask each other questions.

E✗tra practice

Go to this website for more information on how to give seminars and presentations in English: http://ec.hku.hk/tops/ You can watch other students giving presentations.

Can-do checklist

Tick what you can do.

	Can do	Need more practice
I can understand detail in a seminar.		
I can plan and give a mini seminar.		
I can ask questions about a seminar.		

Unit 15
Welcome to the school

Get ready to listen and speak

○ Can you remember your first day at primary school or your first day at an English language school?
Think about the questions below.
What happened on the first day?
Who did you meet?
How did you feel?

go to Useful language p. 81

A Listening – The first day at school

1 🔊 **19** **Anna is the Director of Studies at English Studies International, a language school in London. Listen to her welcoming new students to the school. What is the main reason for her talk? Tick ✓ a, b or c.**

a   to describe the facilities at the school ☐
b   to introduce the English teachers ☐
c   to say what students will do today ☐

2 🔊 **19** **Here are the notes that Anna used for her welcome talk. Listen again and complete the missing information.**

- 9 am: Students do a written test – a ___grammar___ and vocabulary – and a self-assessment. Also have an b _____

- Have a c _____ – about 10.30.

- At 11 am students have introduction to the d _____ Centre.

- Christine gives information about the e _____ programme (11.30 am).

- Students receive f _____ at midday.

- Lunch in the g _____ – students talk to Berit, if they want.

- Afternoon – students have talk or h _____ class.

Did you know ...?
Over 300 languages are spoken in London and there are many different regional accents in the UK.

B Speaking – The first day at school

Speaking strategy
Offering choices

1 Look at these ways of offering choices.

A You can either do the test first or do the self-assessment first.

B This afternoon you could either listen to a talk about London or do a conversation class.

C One option is to visit Madame Tussaud's on Tuesday and another option is to go there at the weekend.

Can you delete the second *do* in A?

YES/NO

Can you delete *do* in B?

YES/NO

Complete the rule.

When the same _____ is used for the two choices, you don't need to _____ it.

Is it possible to replace *can* with *could* in A, and replace *could* with *can* in B?

YES/NO

In C, what word has a similar meaning to *choice*? _____

2 Look at the sentences below.

You can do the test first.

You can do the self-assessment first.

Look at sentence A again. Which two words join the two parts of the sentence?

_____ _____

What word is used to join the two parts of sentence C? _____

Speak up!

3 Use the different ways in *Speaking strategy* to offer choices to a classmate.

Example: a
You say: You can either pay for the social activity now or tomorrow.

a pay for the social activity now / pay tomorrow (*can*)
b do a conversation class in the Learning Centre / in a café (*could*)
c choose the grammar class / ask for extra help in the Learning Centre (*can*)
d borrow a dictionary from the library / buy your own from the bookshop (*could*)
e talk to the Director of Studies about your problem / talk your teacher (*option*)
f stay in the same class / try a higher level (*could*)
g go on the class trip / meet your friends (*can*)
h do your homework in the Learning Centre / do it when you get home (*option*)
i play table tennis / watch the school team play football (*could*)

C Listening – Class rules

1 ⊙ 20 The next day Toby, a teacher, explains some rules to his new students. Listen and complete the missing information on the notice.

2 ⊙ 21 Bruno and Mei Lin are new students at English Studies International, but they are in different classes. Listen to their conversation. Bruno tells Mei Lin one thing that is incorrect. What is it?

_____

Some rules!

- You must ª_____ !
- You must be ᵇ_____ !
- You mustn't use ᶜ_____ !

D Speaking – Class rules

Speaking strategy
Talking about rules

1 Look at what Bruno tells Mei Lin and answer the questions below.

> We have to speak English all the time.

> We aren't allowed to use our mobiles.

a Which sentence says that it is not OK to do something?

----

b Which words in the sentence tell you this?

----

c Which sentence says that it is necessary to do something?

----

d Which words in the sentence tell you this?

----

e Are the rules for all students in Bruno's class?

----

f Did Bruno make the rules or did Toby make the rules?

----

2 Put the words in the correct order to make two questions that Bruno or Mei Lin could ask.

come / we / every / to / have / do / class / to?

----

bring / we / some / are / to / water / class / to / allowed?

3 A new person starts at your school or workplace. Explain the rules to them using the expressions in *Speaking strategy*. You could talk to a friend, or record yourself speaking.

Focus on ...
language of obligation

Toby says:

> You **must** speak English.

> You **mustn't** use your mobile.

The notice says:

> You **must** speak English.

> You **mustn't** use your mobile phone.

Bruno says:

> We **have to** speak English.

> We **aren't allowed to** use our mobile phones.

All the verbs **in bold** talk about things that are necessary.

a Which sounds stronger – *must* or *have to*? *mustn't* or *not allowed to*? ....

b Why does Toby use *must* and *mustn't* when he speaks and in the notice?

----

c Why does Bruno use *have to* and *not allowed to*?

----

d Is it a good idea to use *must* and *mustn't* if the rule is not yours? ....

e Ask if it is necessary to be on time. Use *have to*.

f Ask if it is OK to use your mobile phone. Use *allowed to*.

Note: When you talk about rules, you will be understood if you use any of these expressions, but some sound more natural or more polite.

Learning tip

When you learn new language, it's often important to understand whether the meaning is strong or weak or positive or negative, e.g. *must* is very strong. It is important to understand these meanings so that when you talk you do not give a negative message or sound impolite.

Speak up!

Sound smart
Have to

1 🔊**22** Listen to the pronunciation of *have to* in this sentence.

You have to speak English in class.

Which do you hear? Tick ✓ a, b, c or d.

a /hæv tu/ ☐
b /hæf tu/ ☐
c /hæf tə/ ☐
d /hæv tə/ ☐

2 🔊**23** Listen and repeat the rules from Toby's class. Make sure you pronounce *have to* correctly.

a You have to speak English in class.
b You have to arrive on time.
c You have to turn your mobile phone off.

4 Use the ideas below to explain other rules to Mei Lin.

Example: a
You say: You have to do a test on your first day.

a do / test / first day
b arrive / time / class
c (not) / miss more than 20% of class time
d do / some homework most nights
e do / progress test every month
f bring / coursebook / school every day
g (not) / use / first language in class

5 🔊24 Ask Toby questions about the school rules using *have to* or *be allowed to* and the words below to help you.

Example: a
You say: What time do I have to arrive each day?
You hear: At nine o'clock.

a What time / arrive / each day?
b You: arrive early?
   Toby: Of course. You can wait in the classroom.
c You: How often / do homework?
   Toby: I'll give you some most nights.
d You: bring / coursebook / every day?
   Toby: Yes, you do. We'll use it in class all the time
e You: write / in my coursebook?
   Toby: Yes, of course you are.

Class bonus

What information did you find out on your first day at school or work? Talk about your first day in groups.

E✗tra practice

Go to, or telephone, an English language school and ask in English what happens on the first day of a course. Ask them if they have any special rules about speaking English and doing homework.

Can-do checklist

Tick what you can do.

	Can do	Need more practice
I can understand activities in a timetable.		
I can offer choices.	✓	✓
I can understand and talk about rules.		

Unit 16
What are your goals?

Get ready to listen and speak

○ Think about learning English. What are you good at? What do you need to work on? Number them 1–4 (1 = the one you are best at).

reading ......   listening ......   writing ......   speaking ......

○ What do you like doing in English? What don't you like doing? Number them 1–4 (1 = your favourite).

reading ......   listening ......   writing ......   speaking ......

go to Useful language p. 81

A Listening – Advice session

1 🔵25 **Nigel is Mayuki's English teacher. He gives Mayuki advice about how she can improve her English outside the classroom. Listen and tick ✓ what they talk about.**

reading ☐
listening ☐
writing ☐
speaking ☐
vocabulary ☐
pronunciation ☐
grammar ☐

2 🔵25 **Listen again and complete Nigel's notes. You can write more than one word in each gap.**

Learning tip

Watching TV and movies in English can help you improve your speaking and listening. Use the ideas in Appendix 5 to help you get the most out of watching movies in English.

Student Advisory Session	
Name: Mayuki Nagasaki	
Advisor: Nigel	
What student does:	**Teacher's suggestions:**
• speaks English to a ....._friends_..... but thinks it's difficult to speak English	• don't worry about b ....
• thinks in Japanese and then c	• keep practising speaking. • watch part of a movie three or four times e(.................... minutes)
• watches d .... in English	1st Listening – listen for general meaning
	2nd Listening – understand more f ....
	3rd Listening – use g ....
	4th Listening – listen for h .... and pronunciation

B Speaking – Advice session

Speaking strategy
Giving advice

1 Look at how Nigel gives Mayuki advice on how to improve her listening.

a **I think it's important to** watch DVDs in English.

b **What some students find really useful is to** watch part of a movie.

c **Why not** listen for general meaning only?

d **You could** listen again.

Speak up!

Are the expressions **in bold** suggestions or rules?

Which expression introduces someone else's opinion?

Which expression introduces the speaker's opinion?

2 Maria is learning English. Give her some advice on how to improve her listening by watching DVDs in English. Use the expressions in *Speaking strategy* and the words below to help you.

Example: a
You say: You could watch DVDs in English.
Example: b
You say: I think it's important not to listen for detail the first time.

a could/ watch DVDs English
b important / not / listen for detail the first time
c why / watch five / ten minutes / movie
d first time / listen/ I think / important/ listen/ general information
e important / not use / subtitles / first time
f second time / listen / could / try / understand more detail
g what some students / useful / use / subtitles
h fourth time / why / listen / new words

3 Now give Maria some advice on how to improve her speaking. Use your own ideas and the ideas below.

Example:
You say: I think it's important to talk a lot.

How to improve your speaking
- talk a lot
- ask lots of questions
- don't worry about mistakes
- join a conversation group
- talk to yourself
- record yourself speaking and then listen to it

C Listening – Learning outside the classroom

1 Nigel talks to Mayuki two weeks later. Listen to their conversation.

1 [26] What does Nigel talk about? Listen and tick ✓ a, b or c.
   a the study Mayuki has done in the last two weeks ☐
   b Mayuki's progress ☐
   c what Mayuki can do to improve her English ☐

2 What are Mayuki's learning goals about? Tick ✓ a, b or c.
   a work ☐
   b personal life ☐
   c both ☐

2 [26] Look at the advice sheet Nigel gave Mayuki. Listen again and complete the missing information.

Advice sheet : Planning your learning

Set ^a _____goals_____

e.g. Speaking – on the ^b_____ and in everyday conversations
      Listening – to the news, seminars, ^c_____

Find material

e.g. listening and speaking books in the self access centre, ^d_____
      groups etc.

Ask yourself questions

e.g. What ^e_____?
      How ^f_____?
      Do ^g_____?

Learning tip

Sometimes when you are studying on your own it is difficult to stay motivated. Try doing different things to keep you interested, like studying with a friend or studying online. Planning your learning will also help. See Appendix 6 for ideas on how to do this.

D Speaking – Learning outside the classroom

Speaking strategy
Describing learning goals

Welcome everybody

Before

After

1 **Look at the expressions in bold Mayuki uses to talk about her goals.**

> **My main goal is to** talk to foreign visitors easily when they visit our company.

> **I need to** talk about my job.

> **I want to** talk to people when I go overseas on holiday.

Which expression is stronger? Tick ✓ a or b.

a need to ☐   b want to ☐

2 **Put the letters in the correct order to make three words you can use instead of goal.**

mia   _a_ _i_ _m_
mreda _ _ _ _ _
btmanoii _ _ _ _ _ _ _ _

Speak up!

3 **What are the goals of the students below? Talk about them.**

Example: a
You say: Lucia's dream is to study at university in the US.

a Lucia: study / university / the US   (*dream*)
b Omar: understand lectures / presentations / English (*goal*)
c Stefan: speak English / phone / (*need*)
d Li-Ying: write essays / English (*want*)
e Katerina: speak English / work (*aim*)

4 **What are your most important learning goals? Use the expressions in *Speaking strategy* to talk about them.**

Learning tip

Make your own learning goals and think about what you need to do to achieve them. Talk to your teacher or a friend about your plans. They might have some other ideas to help you.

Class bonus

Talk in small groups about learning English. Do you like doing the same activities in class? Which is your favourite activity? What are your learning goals? Do you want to learn English for the same reasons?

E✗tra practice

Go to the Hong Kong Polytechnic University Centre for Independent Language Learning (CILL) website: http://elc.polyu.edu.hk/cill/ Look at the information and exercises they have to help you improve your listening and speaking.

Can-do checklist

Tick what you can do.

	Can do	Need more practice
I can understand advice on how to improve English.		
I can give people advice on how to learn their English.		
I can talk about my learning goals.		

Review 2
Units 11–16

For each question tick ✓ a, b or c.

1 Which expression does **not** talk about a schedule?
   a Business is very good today. ☐
   b He's going to introduce you to the Finance Director. ☐
   c You'll visit the factory this afternoon. ☐

2 Which expression does **not** talk about the future?
   a I'm planning to increase profits. ☐
   b We'd like to increase profits. ☐
   c We've increased our profits. ☐

3 Which expression talks about something you finished recently?
   a I've put out all the glasses. ☐
   b I'm going to put out all the glasses. ☐
   c I'm putting out all the glasses. ☐

4 Which is the most direct way to ask people to do things?
   a Would you be able to order lunch? ☐
   b I need you to order lunch. ☐
   c Could I ask you to order lunch? ☐

5 What can you say when you start a long talk or seminar?
   a I'm going to talk to you about … ☐
   b The first point is … ☐
   c Another point is … ☐

6 Which is **not** a suitable question to ask about the seminar 'Money and the Internet'?
   a Is online banking safe? ☐
   b What type of sport do you recommend? ☐
   c Can I apply for every account online? ☐

7 Which expression does **not** offer a choice?
   a You can either study grammar or vocabulary. ☐
   b One option is to go to the cinema and another option is to go out for dinner. ☐
   c You must have lunch early. ☐

8 Which expression makes the rule sound the strongest?
   a You must pay a deposit for the course. ☐
   b You should pay a deposit for the course. ☐
   c You have to pay a deposit for the course. ☐

9 Which sentence does **not** describe a goal?
   a My aim is to work for an international company. ☐
   b I need to talk about my job in English. ☐
   c I always study hard in English lessons. ☐

10 Which sentence does **not** give advice?
   a Why not listen again? ☐
   b You must listen again. ☐
   c You could listen again. ☐

Section 2

Answer these questions.

11 Make two sentences about your future plans. Use *plan* and *hope*.

    ----

12 Make this feedback softer.

    Clear the tables faster!

    ----

13 Ask if someone has done something using *yet* and the words below.

    give / them / menu /

    ----

14 What are some things you should listen for when you listen to a recording of yourself giving a seminar?

    ----

15 Write a question using *have to* and the words below.

    come / every lesson

    ----

16 Give some advice using *why not?* and the words below.

    listen / songs / English

    ----

17 What are two things you can do to improve your speaking?

    ----

18 What are two things you can do to improve your listening?

Section 3

🔊 27 Listen and answer these questions.

19 Listen to this description. What is being described?

    ----

20 Listen. Which sentence has the correct stress?

    a The café has chocolate <u>cake</u>, but the shop only has fruit <u>cake</u>.

    b The café has <u>chocolate</u> cake, but the shop only has <u>fruit</u> cake.

21 Listen and reply.

    What's your schedule for today?

22 Listen and reply.

    What are your learning goals?

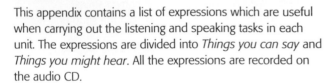

Appendix 1
Useful language

This appendix contains a list of expressions which are useful when carrying out the listening and speaking tasks in each unit. The expressions are divided into *Things you can say* and *Things you might hear*. All the expressions are recorded on the audio CD.

You can use this appendix in the following ways.

Before you begin each unit, do one of the following:
1 Look at the expressions and use your dictionary to check the meaning of any words you do not understand.
2 Look at the expressions, and try to work out the meaning of any words you do not understand *when you see or hear them in the unit*. This is more challenging, but it is a very useful skill to practise.

After you complete each unit:
3 Look at the expressions and check that you understand them. Try to think of different examples using the same key words. Find the key words and expressions in the Audioscript to see them in context.
4 Listen to the expressions, and notice the stress and rhythm of the speaker. You may want to mark sentence stress in a highlighter pen. Listen again and repeat each phrase, practising the stress and rhythm.
5 Listen again to the expressions and notice the pronunciation of any difficult words. You may want to mark word stress in a highlighter pen. Listen once more and repeat each word, practising the word stress.
6 Cover a column, then listen to each expression and repeat from memory. This helps to focus your listening.

Unit 1

Things you can say	Things you might hear
The reason I'm ringing is because it's my birthday.	I'm having a party to celebrate.
I was wondering if you wanted to come.	Have you met Reshma?
That sounds good.	We play football together.
That sounds good but I'm afraid I'm going away.	It's nice food, isn't it?
Do you want me to bring anything?	
What day?	
What time?	
Hello, Brian speaking.	
It's Mark here.	
It's cold today, isn't it?	
What do you do?	
How do you know Mark?	

Unit 2

Things you can say	Things you might hear
Sorry, 36 …	I'll come round and have a look at it.
I was just wondering where it is.	Please leave a message and I'll get back to you as soon as I can.
What size are the bedrooms?	It's a ten-minute walk to the shops.
Is there a garden?	
I'm phoning to let you know …	
I was wondering if you could get someone to come and have a look at it.	
The shower's broken.	
I've lost my keys.	
It's not working.	

Unit 3

Things you can say	Things you might hear
How can I tell if … ? What should I do then / next / after that? Can I get this discount pass from normal ticket machines or from special ticket machines? Can I buy a ticket / card / pass only on Monday or on any day? How does the discount card work?	You need to insert the ticket / card / pass into the machine.

Unit 4

Things you can say	Things you might hear
I don't feel like cooking. What about having Thai food? I've got an idea. Last night I went to a Cambodian restaurant. For a starter / a main course / dessert I had … It was delicious / tasty / spicy / mild. It's made with coconut milk / tomatoes.	It's very similar to Thai, but the flavours aren't quite as strong. It's supposed to be very reasonable. There was a taste of lemon grass / lime leaves / ginger. Did you enjoy it?

Unit 5

Things you can say	Things you might hear
I think my camera was stolen. It's quite a small digital camera. It was in a grey case with a shoulder strap. It's not very old. It's a Nokia. I've got travel insurance.	Can you describe the camera please? What's it like? Do you know what make it is?

Unit 6

Things you can say	Things you might hear
I think I've got the flu. I've got terrible toothache. Oh no. Take some lozenges / painkillers. They will help. You should take … It's a kind of tea. It's a bit like a …	What are your symptoms? Have you got a temperature? Are you coughing?

Unit 7

Things you can say	Things you might hear
Can you recommend somewhere central? It's too expensive for me. What's it like? I'm not keen on sharing a bedroom. Can you tell me more about that? Could I have a look at it?	How about a hostel / hotel / guesthouse? This one here is about 30 bucks for a night. You'll be sharing a bathroom. There are cooking facilities. It's really modern. This is the lounge. It's got a widescreen TV with satellite channels.

Unit 8

Things you can say	Things you might hear
Yeah and how much is that? Oh OK, ah ha. Oh wow. Sounds good / great. I'd like to go skydiving.	Hi, how can I help you? We have a tour every day. I just need a name that I can book under. How do you spell that? I'll just confirm that for you.

Unit 9

Things you can say	Things you might hear
Would it be possible to fly three days later? Could I go in the morning? I'm really tired so I don't want to do more exercise. I don't want to do the cycling trip because I'm really tired.	Let me just check the availability. Can you give me the booking number? If you cancel now, you will lose that deposit. A trip that lots of people do is …

Unit 10

Things you can say	Things you might hear
The weather is getting hotter. There were more / fewer cyclones this year. I'm not an expert … but I think it's getting worse. I think that's because of global warming. In my opinion we can do something about it.	Europe is experiencing a heatwave. Temperatures are rising. How are people making global warming worse? What's causing all this?

Unit 11

Things you can say	Things you might hear
I have our schedule for today. At ten o'clock, in half an hour, you'll meet our CEO. We've arranged a visit tomorrow morning to the plantation. You can visit the factory and look at all the brands. I'm planning to increase profits. I'd like to expand.	Will there be an opportunity to do some tasting? I own three cafés, a small chain. All these high rise buildings – it's like being in New York!

Unit 12

Things you can say	Things you might hear
I've already filled the sugar bowls. I've put them out. Have you folded the napkins yet? There are just a few little things. It was just a little thing. Can you just make sure you clear the plates?	You're very friendly and natural with the customers. They can have some time to just chat a bit. How about tips? How did you do?

Unit 13

Things you can say	Things you might hear
I need you to organise the projector. You'll need to sort out lunch. … a big thing for writing up notes … … some stuff for cleaning the whiteboard … The food is probably nicer / better. Their delivery charge is more expensive. You get much more variety.	Make sure that everyone has a notepad. A flip chart would be really useful. They have gourmet sandwiches not just ordinary sandwiches.

Unit 14

Things you can say	Things you might hear
I'm going to talk to you about … The first point is about … The next point is about … Another important point is … My final tip is … I'd like to ask when you should talk to your employer. I'm interesteed in knowing what kind of bank account you should have. Do you think it's safe to use the Internet for banking?	It's a good idea to borrow money for assets. Try and increase how much you save every year. You have a problem if you spend more money than you earn.

Unit 15

Things you can say	Things you might hear
The first thing is … From 9 am until 10.30 am … And then after that / at 1.30 pm … We have to speak English all the time. We're allowed to bring some water to class.	Self assessment is when you decide / think about your language / level. You could either go to a talk about London or do a conversation class. You mustn't use mobile phones.

Unit 16

Things you can say	Things you might hear
My aim is to study English at university. My dream is to study in the UK. My ambition is to work for an international company. My main goal is to talk to foreign visitors. I need to understand lectures in English.	What sort of things do you want to listen to? I think it's important to watch DVDs in English. First, you need to set some goals. Stop and think about your learning. What some students find really useful is to watch part of a movie. You could listen again.

Appendix 2
Listening learning tips

This is a summary of all the Listening learning tips. The unit number is at the end of each tip so you can look back and see how the tip is linked to the activities you did.

Thinking about how you will listen

- Read the exercise before you listen and make sure you know what you are listening for. For example, is it a number or a word? (Unit 2)

- If you know the topic of a conversation, it is a good idea to think about what you know about that topic before you listen. This makes it easier to understand the conversation. (Unit 10)

Listening for general meaning

- Try and understand the general meaning of a text before you listen for the details. Don't worry if you can't understand everything. Think about what you want to know and only listen for that information. (Unit 1)

- Try to understand the words that are strongly stressed because these are often the most important words. (Unit 10)

Listening for more detail

- Sometimes it's possible to remember information from the first time you listened. Check this information when you listen for the second time. (Unit 4)

- Sometimes it's important to listen very carefully and understand every word. Listening to a short text like this can help you practise listening for details, but it's not a good idea to listen to a long conversation in this way. (Unit 4)

When you check your answers to a listening exercise

- When you check your answers, think about why you got them right or wrong. If you know why you got something wrong, maybe you won't make the same mistake again. (Unit 5)

When you have to listen and understand in a real-world situation

- When you are listening to a CD, you get less information because you can't see the speakers. For example, in a Tourist Information Office, the officer will point to brochures and information inside them. This helps you to understand what he or she is saying. (Unit 8)

- When you listen to people talking, try to listen to how they sound as well as what they say. The tone of their voice can give you useful information about the person's attitude, for example, whether they are feeling positive or negative, or happy or sad. (Unit 12)

- Watching TV and movies in English can help you improve your speaking and listening. Use the ideas in Appendix 5 to help you get the most out of watching movies in English. (Unit 16)

Making a note of new language

- When you hear new expressions or questions, make sure you listen for the words or syllables that are stressed. When you record these words in your notebook, mark the stress by underlining the strongest syllable, e.g. mach<u>ines</u>. (Unit 3)

- It's a good idea to record new words in categories. It helps you to remember them and you can easily add other words to the lists. (Unit 5)

Appendix 3
Speaking learning tips

This is a summary of all the Speaking learning tips. The unit number is at the end of each tip so you can look back and see how the tip is linked to the activities you did.

Preparing to speak

- It's a good idea to practise describing the situation and think about what people might ask you before you have to say it, for example, at the chemist's / post office / bank etc. (Unit 6)

Practising new language

- Don't worry if you don't say the exact same words as the conversation. Try and say something that has a similar meaning. The more you try, the easier it will get. (Unit 1)

- When you learn a new expression, it's a good idea to practise it with different words. (Unit 7)

- Sometimes it's useful to read an example answer aloud, but don't memorize it. Learning to speak from notes rather than reading aloud is difficult, but it helps you get better at speaking freely. (Unit 11)

- Sometimes when you are studying on your own it is difficult to stay motivated. Try doing different things to keep you interested, like studying with a friend or studying online. Planning your learning will also help. See Appendix 6 for ideas on how to do this. (Unit 16)

Thinking about pronunciation

- Some sounds change when they are not stressed, for example:
  can is pronounced /kən/ in I can go this weekend.
  for is pronounced /fə/ in Just for one person. (Unit 8)

Speaking

- Talking on the telephone can be difficult because you can't see who you are talking to.
  To make it easier you can:
  - think about what you will say and how you will say it before you talk on the telephone.
  - think about what the other person might say before you telephone them.
  - repeat part of an answer to check you understand.
  - ask the speaker to repeat things you don't understand and to spell difficult names and addresses. (Unit 2)

- To help keep a conversation going, don't just answer questions, make sure you ask them too. (Unit 5)

- When you give your opinion, it is important to explain your ideas. This helps keep the conversation going and makes it more interesting for the listener. (Unit 10)

- When you give a talk or a seminar, give examples to explain what you mean. This makes it easier for the listener to understand your opinion. (Unit 14)

- Make your own learning goals and think about what you need to do to achieve them. Talk to your teacher or a friend about your plans. They might have some other ideas to help you. (Unit 16)

Making a note of new language

- When you look up a new word in the dictionary, remember to check which syllable is stressed. A ' is put in front of the stressed syllable e.g. noisy /'nɔɪzɪ/. This means the stress is on the first syllable. (Unit 7)

- To help you remember new words, it is useful to use mind maps. Look at the example in Unit 9. (Unit 9)

- When learning useful expressions, it's a good idea to look for patterns or things in common, for example, when you want to talk about completed actions and the time isn't important, we use the pattern:
  I + have + verb   e.g. I've filled … I've put …
  Looking for patterns in language is a useful way of helping you to remember expressions. (Unit 12)

- Thing means the same as 'object'. For materials, liquids or groups of objects we use the word stuff, e.g. some stuff for cleaning the whiteboard. (Unit 13)

- It's often a good idea to record new vocabulary in groups because it makes them easier to remember. Look at the example in Unit 14.

- When you learn new language, it's often important to understand whether the meaning is strong or weak or positive or negative, e.g. must is very strong. It is important to understand these meanings so that when you talk you do not give a negative message or sound impolite. (Unit 15)

Appendix 4
Listening to the news

Listening to the news

It is a good idea to do Unit 10 before you use this worksheet.

Listen to the news in English and use this worksheet to help you understand it. You can listen on the:
- Internet – try these sites: http://www.voanews.com/specialenglish
  http://www.bbc.co.uk/worldservice/learningenglish/newsenglish/index.shtml http://edition.cnn.com/services/podcasting
- Radio – record it so you can listen to it two or three times.
- TV – record it so you can listen to it two or three times.

Listening

1 **Listen to the news. How many different news stories are there?** ....

2 **Listen again and tick ✓ the topics the stories are about.**

national news ☐	international news ☐	politics ☐	crime ☐
disaster ☐	environment ☐	entertainment ☐	health ☐
sport ☐	business ☐	lifestyle ☐	science ☐
media ☐			

3 **Listen again and take notes to fill in the table. Not everything will be in each story so don't worry if you can't write something in every box.**

	Story 1	Story 2	Story 3
What			
When			
Who			
How			
Why			

Speaking

1 **Record yourself describing the news story. Listen to the recording. Have you included all the information above?**

2 **Tell someone (in English) about one of the stories you listened to.**

Extra

Choose one of the stories and find out more information about it. Look at different websites and newspapers to get extra information.

Appendix 5
Watching movies

Watching movies

Use this worksheet whenever you watch movies in English. If you're just watching part of a movie, you can use the activities on the next page *Watching a scene from a movie*.

Get ready to **listen and speak**

Think about these questions.

What do you know about the movie?	What it is about?	When is it?	Who is in it?
What happens?	Where is it?	What kind of movie is it (romance, comedy, thriller, action …)?	

A Listening

As you watch the movie, fill in the three tables below. Get information from what you *see* as well as from what you hear.

1 What are the main events of the film?

Main events	Details (why, when, how, what, who)
e.g. Lola and Patrick meet	on the train, he helped her when someone stole her bag…….

2 Who are the characters? Choose two and complete the table with information about them.

	1	2
Name		
Job		
Personality (e.g. friendly)		
Other details (e.g. family, plans …)		

3 As you watch, write down one to five words you don't know and think are interesting or useful. Try and guess the meaning. After the movie, check your ideas in a dictionary and record the words.

Word	I think it means …	Meaning

B Speaking

1 Talk for one to two minutes about what you think of the movie. Think about what you will say before you speak. You could talk about the actors, story, ending, special effects, scenery, clothes …

2 Find someone who has seen the movie and ask them (in English) what they think about it.

Extra

Find out more about the movie or read a review of it. You could look in an English newspaper/magazine or these sites on the internet: http://www.mrqe.com/ or http://www.imdb.com/ or http://movies.go.com/reviews

Watching a scene from a movie

C Listening

1 Watch a short part of the movie and answer the questions below.
   a Which characters are in the scene? _____
   b Where is the scene? _____
   c What is the feeling or mood in the scene? Tick ✓ the best description.
   romantic ☐   funny ☐   scary ☐   sad ☐   interesting ☐

2 Watch the scene again and take notes.
   a What does each character want to do in this scene?
   Character name: _____ wants to _____
   Character name: _____ wants to _____
   Character name: _____ wants to _____

   b What happens in the scene?
   _____
   _____

3 Watch the scene again and find one line of dialogue that you like in the scene. Write down exactly what the character says.
   _____
   _____

D Speaking

Use the notes you made above to talk about the scene. Record what you say or talk to a friend about it. Start like this:

In (movie name) there is a scene that I like / that it very important / that is very interesting. The scene takes place in …

Appendix 6
What's next?

It is a good idea to plan what you will study next. Use this worksheet to plan how you can improve your listening and speaking.

1 What is your most important listening or speaking goal?

Example: I want to improve my speaking so I can talk to friends in English about everyday topics.

Complete this sentence about your goal.

I want to improve my .... so I can ....

2 How can you achieve this goal? Write a list of things you will do. You could use some of the ideas in the Extra tasks in each unit.

Things I will do
— record myself talking for a minute every day about everyday topics
— listen to conversations on TV, in movies or in public places like on the bus (Extra Unit 1)
— ....
— ....
— ....
— ....

3 After you have done the things on your list, think about what you learned. Answer these questions:

What did I learn?

....

How useful was it?

....

Do I need to change anything next time?

....

4 Now do the same for your other learning goals.

Audioscript

These recordings are mostly in standard British English. Where a speaker has a different accent, it is noted in brackets.

Unit 1

2 (Mark = American)
Brian: Hello, Brian speaking.
Mark: Hi Brian. It's Mark here.
Brian: Hi Mark. How are you?
Mark: I'm fine. How are you?
Brian Fine.
Mark: I haven't caught you at a bad time, have I?
Brian: No, no. I was just watching TV.
Mark: Oh good. Have you had a good weekend?
Brian: Yeah, I went to the cinema with some friends yesterday. I haven't done much today. Just at home ... watching TV. Yeah, it's been good. What about you?
Mark: Yeah not too bad. Hey, actually the reason I'm ringing is because it's my birthday next week ...
Brian: Oh OK, yeah.
Mark: ... and um I thought I might have a few people round at the weekend to celebrate and I was wondering if you wanted to come.
Brian: That sounds good. What day?
Mark: Saturday, Saturday night.
Brian: Saturday. Yeah, yeah. I don't have any plans for next Saturday. Great. What time?
Mark: Um, about 7.30.
Brian: OK. But I don't think I can get there till 8 o'clock.
Mark: No problem.
Brian Do you want me to bring anything?
Mark: No nothing. I'll get the food and everything.
Brian: OK. Do you want anything special for your birthday?
Mark: No. No you don't have to buy a birthday present. Just come along and help me celebrate. That's all.
Brian: OK. That sounds great.
Mark: See you on Saturday.
Brian: Cool. See you then.
Mark: Bye for now.
Brian: Bye.

3
Mark called last night. It's his birthday next week and he's having a party on Saturday to celebrate. It starts at 7.30. He doesn't want me to take anything. I'm looking forward to it.

4
What day?

5
a Do you want me to bring anything?
b What time?
c That sounds good.

6 (Mark = American)

Mark: Hi. It's Mark here.

Mark: I'm fine. How are you?

Mark: Have you had a good weekend?

Mark: Not too bad. Actually the reason I'm ringing is because it's my birthday next week and I'm going to have a party. I was wondering if you wanted to come.

Mark: Saturday night.

Mark: About 7.30.

Mark: No. I'll have food and everything.

Mark: See you on Saturday. Bye.

7
Brian: Hello, Brian speaking.

Brian: Hi. How are you?

Brian: Fine.

Brian: Yes I have. I went to the cinema with some friends yesterday and I haven't done much today. What about you?

Brian: That sounds good. What day?

Brian: OK. What time?

Brian: Do you want me to bring anything?

Brian: OK. That sounds great. See you then.

Brian: Bye.

8 (Mark = American; Reshma = Indian)
Mark: Hey Brian, have you met Reshma?
Brian: No I haven't.
Mark: Oh OK. Reshma, this is Brian.
Reshma: Hello ... um ... sorry, what was your name?
Brian: Brian.
Reshma: Brian. Hi. I'm Reshma.
Brian: Hi Reshma.
Mark: Brian and I play football together.
Reshma: Oh OK. Is your team doing well?
Mark: Yeah ... well ... we lost last week but we usually win most of our games.
Brian: Yeah, we're doing really well actually ...
Mark: Hey, I'll be back in a minute guys. A few more people have just arrived so I'd better go and say hi.
Reshma: OK.

(pause)

Brian: How do you know Mark?
Reshma: Um I live next door ...
Brian: OK.
Reshma: So I've known him since he moved in, um, a couple of years ago I guess.
Brian: OK.

9
A: So what do you do?
B: Ah I work for Trust Savings Bank.
A: Oh OK. And ah what do you do there?
B: I work in customer services. Yeah I help people set up new accounts and that kind of thing.
A: Oh OK. Do you like it?
B: Yeah it's not bad. It's a good company to work for ... What about you? What do you do?
A: I'm a shop assistant. I sell mobile phones.

10
A: It's cold today, isn't it?
B: Freezing.
A: They say this has been the coldest winter in 30 years.

B: Really? No wonder I've felt cold. Do you think it'll snow?

A: Maybe. That'd be really strange though because it hasn't snowed here in years.

B: Mmm, it's weird how the weather's changing. I think …

🔵 11

What do you do?

The food's good, isn't it?

How long have you lived here?

Do you know anyone here?

This is a nice house, isn't it?

It's cold today, isn't it?

Unit2

🔵 12 (Landlord = New Zealander)

Landlord: Hello.

Susan: Ah hello. I'm phoning about the house in Glen Eden that's advertised in the paper today.

Landlord: Yes.

Susan: I was just wondering where it is exactly.

Landlord: 36 Arawa Street.

Susan: Sorry, 36 …

Landlord: Arawa Street, A-R-A-W-A. It's number 36.

Susan: Oh OK. The ad says it's close to the shopping centre and train station. How far away are they?

Landlord: Yeah, it's really close. Um, it's probably about a ten-minute walk to the shops and five minutes to the train station, so it's not far from anything.

Susan: Oh good. Um, the bedrooms. There are two, aren't there? What size are they?

Landlord: Yeah, one's a bit bigger than the other … um but they're … about … medium size I guess.

Susan: Would they both fit double beds in them?

Landlord: Ah the bigger one would, but the other one probably only fits a single bed. Ah they're both very sunny rooms.

Susan: Oh OK. Is there a garden?

Landlord: Ah not really. There's a small area where you can hang your washing, but no garden … You can go and have a look at it if you want.

Susan: OK, yeah.

Landlord: And your name is?

Susan: Susan.

Landlord: OK Susan, if you're interested, I'll be down there at 5.30 if you want to come and have a look.

Susan: Oh OK, thanks … Bye.

Landlord: Bye.

🔵 13

Sorry, 36 …

🔵 14 (Landlord = New Zealander)

Landlord: It's in Arawa Street.

Susan: What was that?

Landlord: Arawa Street.

Landlord: It's in Arawa Street.

Susan: Pardon?

Landlord: Arawa Street.

🔵 15 (Landlord = New Zealander)

a Landlord: The other bedroom probably only fits a single bed.

----

b Landlord: Um, it's probably about a ten-minute walk to the shops.

----

c Landlord: OK, if you're interested I'll be down there at 5.30.

🔵 16

Sorry, the other bedroom fits a …

Sorry, it's a ten-minute walk to …

Sorry, you'll be down there at …

🔵 17

I was just wondering where it is.

🔵 18

a I was just wondering how far it is.

b I was just wondering how much it is.

c I was just wondering how many bedrooms there are.

d I was just wondering when I can move in.

🔵 19 (Landlord = New Zealander)

Landlord: Hello, Tony speaking.

Susan: Ah hi, it's Susan from your flat in Arawa Street here.

Landlord: Oh hi Susan. What can I do for you?

Susan: Um, we've got a bit of a problem in the flat. The oven's not working … I was cooking dinner last night and I had some stuff in the oven. After a while I realized it wasn't cooking. The oven was on, but it wasn't getting hot. I had a look at the plug, thinking it might be that, but that

seems to be OK … I'm not sure why … but it's not working … I was wondering if you could get someone to come and have a look at it for us.

Landlord: Ah … Was it working before yesterday?

Susan: Yeah, it's been working fine, but for some reason we couldn't get it going last night … We use it quite a lot so it would be good if we could get it fixed.

Landlord: Ah … OK … Um, I'll come round and have a look and see if I can fix it. If I can't, I'll get an electrician in.

Susan: OK.

Landlord: Ah … I won't be able to come til tomorrow night. Say about seven. Will someone be home then?

Susan: Ah yeah. I'll be here.

Landlord: OK. Well I'll have a look at it tomorrow.

Susan: OK then. See you about seven.

Landlord: Yeah OK … Bye.

Susan: OK Bye.

🔵 20

Hello, it's Susan from your flat in Arawa Street. I'm phoning to let you know there's a broken window. We can't close it and it's really cold! Could you please send someone around to fix it? Thanks. Bye.

🔵 21 (Landlord = New Zealander)

Hello, you've reached Tony Goodman. I can't take your call right now, so please leave a message and I'll get back to you as soon as I can. Thanks.

Unit3

🔵 22 (Kumiko = Japanese)

Matt: Hello, I'd like to get some information about catching the underground, please.

Kumiko: Yes, of course.

Matt: Well, the first thing I'm not sure about is umm … how do I buy a ticket?

Kumiko: Ah yes. Well, to begin, you should look for a ticket machine – you can find them at the station.

Matt: OK.

Kumiko: And um you can … you can use coins or notes.

Matt: Any coins or notes?

Kumiko: With coins only 500 yen and 100 and 50 and ten.

Matt: Hmm. OK.

Kumiko: You can use 1,000 yen notes in every machine.

Matt: I see.

Kumiko: And you can also find some

machines where you can use 5,000 and 10,000 yen notes.

Matt: How will I know which notes I can use?

Kumiko: It will say on the machine. And some take credit card* too.

Matt: So how much money … How can I tell how much money I need to put in the machine?

Kumiko: There's a map which tells you. It's above the machine.

Matt: Oh right – the big map.

Kumiko: Yes. You can find the price. You have to … er you need to choose the correct price for the place you want to go to.

Matt: Ah right – I choose the price. What should I do next? Just catch the train?

Kumiko: Yes, you keep ticket* and insert it in the machine at the ticket gate.

Matt: And will the ticket come out of the machine?

Kumiko: Yes, it comes out of the machine. So you have to keep your ticket until you get off.

Matt: And then what do I do? Give the ticket to somebody or … ?

Kumiko: No, when you arrive at the station, you have to insert the ticket into a machine again.

Matt: Oh. OK, at the exit ticket gate?

Kumiko: Yes, the exit ticket gate. But your ticket will not come out.

Matt: OK. I understand. Thank you.

Kumiko: You're welcome.

☞**Did you notice?**

Kumiko says: *And some take credit card too.* A native speaker would say: *And some take credit cards too.*

Kumiko says: *You keep ticket and insert it in the machine.* A native speaker would say: *You keep the ticket and insert it in the machine.*

🔘 **23**

1 Two hundred and fifty
2 Five thousand two hundred
3 Five thousand two hundred and fifty
4 A thousand

🔘 **24** (Kumiko = Japanese)

a Kumiko: Some ticket machines take both notes and coins.

Kumiko: It will say on the machine.

b Kumiko: You put the money in the machine.

Kumiko: You can see on the map.

c Kumiko: You get the ticket from the machine.

Kumiko: Go to the ticket gate.

d Kumiko: You put the ticket in the machine.

Kumiko: Remember to take it when it comes out of the machine.

e Kumiko: You can use credit cards in some stations.

Kumiko: It will say on the machine.

🔘 **25** (Kumiko = Japanese)

Matt: What about discount tickets? Is there any way to get a cheaper fare?

Kumiko: Well, we've only got one discount ticket.

Matt: OK.

Kumiko: If you take the train every Friday or the 20th of every month …

Matt: Mmm.

Kumiko: … you can use the 'No-My-Car-Day' discount pass.

Matt: OK, so how does that work?

Kumiko: If you buy a 'No-My-Car-Day' discount pass, you can go everywhere on the underground for a whole day. And it costs 250 yen less than a normal day pass.

Matt: That sounds good.

Kumiko: But it's only available every Friday or the 20th of every month.

Matt: So you can only get it on those days?

Kumiko: Yes.

Matt: Do I get this discount pass from normal ticket machines or from special ticket machines?

Kumiko: You can buy them from all stations, from all ticket machines.

Matt: OK right – the normal ticket machine. OK.

Kumiko: But if you travel every day, you can get the pre-pay Rainbow Card. You cannot get a discount with it, but it's very useful because you don't need to buy a ticket before you get on the train.

Matt: So how often do I need to buy a Rainbow Card?

Kumiko: Not each morning – perhaps only once a week.

Matt: OK.

Kumiko: So that … for example, on Monday you can buy* 5,000 yen Rainbow Card.

Matt: So how long can I use a 5,000 yen card for?

Kumiko: Ah but it depends on … depends on where you go on the train.

Matt: OK. So will the money come off the card?

Kumiko: Yes, yes.

Matt: So how does it work with the ticket machine at the gate? The same as a normal ticket?

Kumiko: Yes, exactly the same.

Matt: OK. Thank you very much.

Kumiko: You're welcome.

☞**Did you notice?**

Kumiko says: *you can buy 5,000 yen Rainbow card.* A native speaker would say: *you can buy a 5,000 yen Rainbow card.*

🔘 **26**

Do I get this discount pass from normal ticket machines or from special ticket machines?

🔘 **27**

a Do I buy a Rainbow Card from a normal machine or a special machine?
b Do I buy a discount card from all stations or only some stations?
c Do I buy a Rainbow Card only on Monday or any day?
d Do I buy a 500 yen card or a 1,000 yen card?
e Do I get a discount of 200 yen or 250 yen?
f Do I use a Rainbow Card at the usual ticket gate or at a special ticket gate?

🔘 **28** (Kumiko = Japanese)

a ---

Kumiko: They're near all the stations.

b ---

Kumiko: Yes, you can use them in some machines.

c ---

Kumiko: It will say on the machine.

d ---

Kumiko: Yes, you can buy a 'No-My-Car-Day' discount ticket on Fridays.

e ---

Kumiko: Every Friday and on the 20th of every month.

Unit 4

🔘 **29**

Neil: So shall we go out for dinner?

Rachel: Yeah!

Neil: I don't feel like cooking. What about you?

Rachel: I'm tired – I don't want to cook either.

Neil: No. No exactly. So what kind of food do you want?

Rachel: Indian?

Neil: OK, yeah, well er that's what we had last time, so it'd be nice to have something different this time, wouldn't it? What about having Thai food?

Rachel: Oh I'm getting a bit bored with Thai.

Neil: Are you? OK.

Rachel: I've got an idea. There's this new Cambodian restaurant on Queen Street.

Neil: Cambodian? Oh yeah, it's just opened, hasn't it?

Rachel: Yeah … the new one … Ah what's it called? That's right … the Khmer Café.

Neil: I've never tried Cambodian food.

Rachel: Apparently it's very similar to Vietnamese and Thai, but the flavours aren't quite as strong.

Neil: OK.

Rachel: Well, that's what they say. And it has very little meat. Meat is more often used as flavouring.

Neil: OK, so there are a lot of vegetables?

Rachel: A lot of vegetables.

Neil: Well, I suppose we could try that for a change. Why not? And you said it was on Queen Street?

Rachel: That's right – it's a new place and it's supposed to be very reasonable.

Neil: Do you know anyone who's been there?

Rachel: Ah … there was a review in the paper which was positive. Said it wasn't cheap, but it wasn't too expensive and … ah What else did they say? Umm … oh good food and nice and clean … nice atmosphere.

Neil: OK. Let's try that then.

🔘 30

1 Shall we go out for dinner?
2 What about going out for dinner?
3 We could go out for dinner.

🔘 31

I went to the Khmer Café for dinner last Friday night and the food was great. For a starter, I had mushroom soup. It was very simple, but full of flavour. There was a taste of lime leaves and lemon grass together with mushrooms. Then for a main, I had a chicken curry parcel – the Cambodian name is 'amok moan'. At the restaurant, they used cabbage leaves to wrap up the chicken, but in Cambodia they usually use banana leaves. This dish was full of flavours and was delicious. It's made with lemongrass, curry, ginger as well as a little bit of fish sauce. This is all mixed together with coconut milk and the chicken is cooked in this mixture, then wrapped in the cabbage leaves to make the parcels. The waitress told me that

they then steam the parcels for about an hour, then serve with rice.

🔘 32

I went to the Khmer Café for dinner on Friday. For a starter, I had shrimp soup. There was a taste of coconut and lime. It was quite salty. Then for a main course, I had beef stir-fry. It's made with pineapple and tomatoes. This dish was very spicy. For a dessert, I had fried bananas and ice cream. It was delicious.

🔘 33

a When did you last go to a restaurant?
b What type of restaurant was it?
c Did you have a starter? What was it?
d Did you have a dessert? What was it?
e What did you eat for the main course?
f What's it made with?
g Did you enjoy it?

Unit 5

🔘 34 (Arnaud = French)

David: Hi Arnaud. How are you? How was your weekend?

Arnaud: Er, not too good actually. I went to the football game and I caught the bus. And unfortunately on the way back, I left my camera on the bus.

David: Oh no.

Arnaud: And what I …

David: Did you get it back?

Arnaud: No, I didn't. I rang the bus company and they said that they … I gave them the bus number and everything. They said it wasn't there so … It wasn't at the lost property office so, so, no I didn't get it back. I think someone must've taken it.

David: Oh that's terrible. You should, er, you should go to the police.

Arnaud: Yeah do you think that's going to do any good?

David: Yeah I think you've … if you've got insurance you need to go to the police station and report it missing.

Arnaud: Mmm.

David: If you want I could come with you.

Arnaud: OK.

David: When do you want to go? When's good for you?

Arnaud: Well I'm, I'm, free now. Are you?

David: I have to go to the bank but give me ten minutes and I'll meet you at the café down the road.

Arnaud: OK.

David: I'll see you in ten.

Arnaud: OK, see you then.

🔘 35 (Arnaud = French)

David: And how was the rest of your weekend, Arnaud?

Arnaud: Not bad thanks. How was yours?

David: Good. I went out for dinner with some friends on Saturday. I heard there was a free concert in the park but I didn't go. Did you?

Arnaud: No, I didn't. It was too cold. I went to the movies instead.

David: Oh yeah. What did you see?

Arnaud: *Star Wars*. They were showing the second one. It was great. Have you seen it?

David: No, I haven't, but I'd like to. I've only seen the first one.

🔘 36

David: And how was the rest of your weekend, Arnaud?

David: Good. I went out for dinner with some friends on Saturday. I heard there was a free concert in the park but I didn't go. Did you?

David: Oh yeah. What did you see?

David: No, I haven't, but I'd like to. I've only seen the first one.

🔘 37

a How was your weekend?
b What was the last movie you saw?
c What was it like?
d When did you last go on holiday?
e Who did you go with?
f Did you have a good time?

🔘 38

Did you get it back?

🔘 39

a Did you have a good weekend?
b What did you do?
c Did you go to the cinema?
d What did you see?
e Did you like the film?
f Did you go with friends?

🔘 40

a I did.
b I didn't.

🔘 41

a Did you have a good weekend?
b Did you go to the cinema?
c Did you watch football?
d Did you meet your friends?
e Did you study?

🔊 **42** (Arnaud = French)

Officer: Morning.

Arnaud: Hello.

Officer: How can I help?

Arnaud: Well I think my camera was stolen on the bus. I've tried the bus people but they say they don't have it … and er I've got travel insurance.

Officer: OK, yes. Well we need to fill out one of these forms. Um and your name please?

Arnaud: Arnaud Lafayette.

Officer: Arnaud?

Arnaud: Lafayette. L-A-F-A-Y-E-T-T-E.

Officer: Hmm. And what's your address?

Arnaud: Here or in my country?

Officer: Here. Your address in the UK.

Arnaud: 27 Park Road, Birmingham.

Officer: Thank you … And the postcode?

Arnaud: B13 4TY.

Officer: Ah ha. And your phone number?

Arnaud: 07901 672301.

Officer: OK, that's a mobile. Do you have a landline number or email address?

Arnaud: Er, my email's Arnaud L one at hotmail dot com. That's all lower case.

Officer: Great. Now um … so where did you lose your camera?

Arnaud: Well I was on the bus, on the number 16 bus, coming back from a football game.

Officer: 16 bus, OK and, er, when was that?

Arnaud: That was on Saturday morning at about 11 o'clock.

Officer: OK. 11 am. So now can you describe the camera to me please? What's it like?

Arnaud: Well, it's quite a small digital camera. It's in a grey case with a shoulder strap.

Officer: Do you know what make it is?

Arnaud: It's a Nikon. It's not very old. And it's got my name inside.

Officer: OK … ah can you sign here please? Keep this form because your insurance company will want to see it.

Unit 6

🔊 **43** (Chu Hua = Chinese)

Pharmacist: Hello.

Chu Hua: Hi, um I think I've got the flu. Could you, um, could you give me something for it?

Pharmacist: OK um … what are your symptoms?

Chu Hua: Well …

Pharmacist: Have you got a headache, sore throat, temperature? Are you coughing?

Chu Hua: Yeah, I can't stop coughing at night.

Pharmacist: OK … ah … How long have you had the cough?

Chu Hua: Oh erm … um a couple of days now. And I have a headache too.

Pharmacist: Do you take any other medicine?

Chu Hua: No.

Pharmacist: OK. Um … this is cough mixture. It will stop the cough. The most important thing is … take two spoonfuls three or four times a day. Don't take it just when you've got a cough because then it takes a little while to work. You need to take it before you cough … Um … or if you don't want to take medicine, then there is a lozenge you can have. Take two. Have one and then as soon as you finish, take another one. One after the other.

Chu Hua: Can I take both the lozenges and the cough mixture?

Pharmacist: No, no. You must take one or the other. You can have the cough mixture at night time and carry the lozenges in your bag during the day. If you're going to the movies, and you think that cough's going to annoy people, you can have some lozenges. They soothe your throat, because sometimes if your throat's dry, you cough. So that will help there.

Chu Hua: Um, and what about my headache?

Pharmacist: You should take paracetamol for your headache. It's gentle on the stomach and it's safe to take. And … er take two of those every four hours. Maximum of eight in 24 hours. You mustn't take more than that.

Chu Hua: OK. And what about my eyes? They're really sore. Is there anything I can take for them?

Pharmacist: Yes, try these eye drops. Squeeze one or two drops into each eye twice a day.

Chu Hua: OK. And how long do I take this medicine for?

Pharmacist: About ten days. You shouldn't take it for longer than that. OK, and remember to take multivitamins too.

🔊 **44**

You need to take it before you cough.
You should take paracetamol.
Don't take it when you cough.
You shouldn't take it for longer than that.
You mustn't take more than that.

🔊 **45**

a I've got a terrible toothache.

----

b I think I'm getting a cold. I've got a really sore throat.

----

c My knee is really sore and it's very swollen.

----

d I've been working at the computer all day and my eyes are very sore.

----

e I don't feel very well and I've got a headache.

----

f I feel terrible because I can't stop coughing.

🔊 **46** (Ali = Saudi Arabian, Seiji = Japanese, Ana = Brazilian)

Ali: In Saudi Arabia what you do if you have the flu is you drink babunej. It's a kind of hot drink. It's made with camomile, which is a herb. You drink it very hot and sometimes you have it with lots of lemon. You get vitamin C from that.

Seiji: In Japan if you have a sore throat, we use daikon, a Chinese radish. It's a bit like a large white carrot. We grind the Chinese radish and put honey on it and leave it for a while. Then we wait until the juice comes out … and then we drink it.

Ana: In Brazil if you're not well … you've got a cold or flu or something like that … well, garlic is really important. You have a glass of water and you put a little garlic in it and mix it together. Every half hour, you drink two or three spoonfuls of the liquid. I don't know if it works but we try it.

Unit 7

🔊 **47** (Anke = German; Dan = Canadian)

Anke: I've just arrived here in Vancouver. I'm looking for somewhere to stay.

Dan: What kind of accommodation would you like?

Anke: Can you recommend somewhere central? Near to the city, the shops – yeah.

Dan: OK, well, ah … let's have a look. How about this one? The Pioneer. It's right in the centre of town. It's nice – it's comfortable, you get your own room and bathroom. So, what do you think?

Anke: How much are we talking about?

Dan: Well, it's about 200 dollars a night. But that includes breakfast.

Anke: Oh, it's too expensive for me.

Dan: Ah, OK, all right. So, let's have a look at something a bit cheaper here. Let's see, well here are some more hotels. They're all quite central and comfortable.

Anke: How much are they?

Dan: Well, the cheapest hotel is … let's see, The Vancouver Inn – this one's 110 bucks. It includes breakfast, and all the rooms have a bathroom so that's good.

Anke: Oh, it's still a bit too expensive for me.

Dan: OK. How about a hostel? This one here – BC Lodge – you see, it's 30 bucks for a night.

Anke: What's it like?

Dan: Well, it's fairly typical. It's got shared bedrooms and you'll be sharing a bathroom, of course. There are cooking facilities – you can cook stuff there, but breakfast is provided. It's fun, it's lively – good atmosphere.

Anke: Ah OK. Yeah so … it's a better price for me, but I'm not keen on sharing a bedroom. And I can pay a little more than 30 dollars – no problem.

Dan: OK. Oh well, I know just the thing. Here we go. This is a guesthouse, The Maple Leaf Villa.

Anke: And what about the price?

Dan: 60 bucks a night. That's good – that's a good price, yeah. Cheaper than the hotels.

Anke: That sounds interesting. Can you tell me more about that?

Dan: It's very central – it's actually an historic building. Here's a photo. And you can see here that you get your own room. The bathroom's shared, but that's not so bad. You can see it's very comfortable.

Anke: Yeah, it looks good. OK, maybe a good place for me. Could I have a look at it?

●48

noisy   quiet

●49

noisy   quiet   hotel   central   luggage
private   hostel

●50

expensive   convenient   interesting
possible

●51 (Dan = Canadian)

Dan: Hello. Can I help you?

Dan: Hi there. How can I help you?

Dan: How about the Vancouver Inn? It's $110 a night.

Dan: You could try a hostel.

Dan: How about this guesthouse (*pause*) The Maple Leaf Villa? It's very central, but it's not too expensive.

●52 (Ray = Canadian)

Why don't you come on in? Come this way. OK so this is the lounge. It's fairly big. It's got a widescreen TV and we get about 30 satellite channels and, as you can see, it's pretty comfortable.

This is the kitchen. You share it with other guests and, as you can see, it's recently been renovated. There's a microwave and fridge for you to use. You can either cook your own breakfast or we'll prepare it and bring it to your room.

This is one of the bedrooms. This is a basic room and it costs 60 bucks a night, which is quite cheap. As you can see, it's got a really big bed. It's got a sink, a desk and this very comfortable chair here.

Here's the bathroom. You share with just one other guest. There's a power shower and plenty of towels. I think you can see, it's a comfortable place to stay.

Unit8

●53 (Amy = New Zealander)

Amy: Hi, how can I help you?

Calum: Um I'm wondering, um I've just arrived in Auckland and I'm looking for information … ah … what can I do here? What is there to see?

Amy: Sure. What kind of things are you interested in?

Calum: Um I heard about … ah the dolphins. Can you see dolphins near here?

Amy: Yes you can do that in Auckland er that's basically a full-day trip. Usually … starting at about eleven through till about four o'clock, so you would need most of your day to do that.

Calum: Yeah and how much is that?

Amy: That is … 40 dollars.

Calum: Ah ha.

Amy: And they go every day.

Calum: Oh all right. And do you see dolphins every time?

Amy: Yes … well not absolutely guaranteed, not 100 percent, but they do … most of the time they will see dolphins or … it may be whales.

Calum: Oh wow.

Amy: At this time of the year you can see different kinds of whales.

Calum: Sounds good …

Amy: We also have adventure activity things to do.

Calum: Yeah? What are the adventure activities?

Amy: All sorts. You can go bungy jumping. You jump off the harbour bridge. It's 45 metres high and it costs 85 dollars. It's very popular.

Calum: OK.

Amy: Er … you can go skydiving.

Calum: Skydiving!

Amy: Yes you go up to over 3,000 metres, 45 seconds free fall. It's …

Calum: I've always wanted to do that but … is it expensive?

Amy: It's … ah 250 dollars.

Calum: Ah ha. OK. What are the other options? Not so dangerous.

Amy: There's the underwater world just six kilometres from the centre of Auckland. It's an aquarium where the fish are swimming around on top of you.

Calum: OK yeah, great.

Amy: They're open until 7 pm. And that's 16 dollars.

Calum: OK. Ah … I'd like to think about it and …

Amy: Of course. Here are the brochures. Just let me know if you have any more questions.

●54

oh all right

●55

a   ah ha
b   ok
c   oh wow
d   sounds good
e   yeah
f   great

●56

a   You can see dolphins and whales.

----

b   We have a tour every day.

----

c   It's a good idea to take your camera.

----

d   Usually it costs $140 but it's only $100 today.

----

e   You need to take your own lunch.

----

f   There are sometimes more than 50 dolphins.

🔘57 (Amy = New Zealander)

Amy: Hello again. Have you decided what you'd like to do?

Calum: I'd like to go skydiving. Can I book that here or … ?

Amy: Yes, yes. If you want us to make a booking we would be happy to um …

Calum: Yep, that'd be great. I think I'll do that now while I'm here.

Amy: OK, well … we just need to get a few details from you. First of all we need to know what day you want to go. They do it seven days a week so you just need to choose a day.

Calum: Well the weekend is better. Saturday.

Amy: OK. Which Saturday would you like?

Calum: Ah, I can go this weekend.

Amy: This weekend?

Calum: Yeah.

Amy: OK and if the Saturday isn't available, is Sunday OK?

Calum: Yeah, fine.

Amy: OK, so that's the 29th or 30th?

Calum: Yes.

Amy: Just for one person? Or do you have a friend who you think might want to come?

Calum: Ah no just me.

Amy: OK … and I just need a name that I can book under.

Calum: Calum.

Amy: How do you spell that?

Calum: C-A-L-U-M.

Amy: Ah-ha and I just need your last name as well.

Calum: Brodie. B-R-O-D-I-E.

Amy: OK so I'll make that booking. You'll need to pay here. Is that OK?

Calum: Yep. Do I get a student discount? I'm a university student.

Amy: Ah, yes, you do.

Calum: Oh great.

Amy: So with the discount it's 200 dollars.

Calum: OK, thanks.

Amy: I'll just confirm that online, if you'd like to wait a minute.

Calum: OK.

Amy: Oh I'm sorry. The weekend's fully booked. What about Thursday or Friday?

Calum: I'll go on Friday then.

Amy: That's the 28th of March. One moment … OK, that's all booked for you. You just give your name when you go there. Here's a map that shows you how to get there. It's very easy to find.

🔘58

I'd like to go skydiving.

🔘59

a he'd
b she'd
c it'd
d we'd
e they'd

🔘60

I wouldn't like to go skydiving.

🔘61

a What did you decide to do?

----

b What day do you want to go?

----

c For how many people?

----

d Can you give me your full name?

----

e How do you spell your surname?

----

f And I just need a contact telephone number as well.

Thank you. I'll just confirm that for you.

Unit9

🔘62 (Helen = South African)

Helen: Good afternoon, sir. How can I help you?

Adam: Yes, hello. I'd like to change my flight to Cape Town.

Helen: Hmm. OK, so can you tell me the booking number?

Adam: Umm … I don't remember my booking number, to be honest.

Helen: OK. That's OK. Maybe just your family name then. Can you give me that?

Adam: Yeah, my family name is Lister.

Helen: Is that L-I-S-T-E-R?

Adam: That's right. Adam Lister.

Helen: OK, let me just check that for you.

Adam: The airline is South African Airlines and I think the flight number is SAA 235.

Helen: Great. And when are you flying?

Adam: Oh, it's next Monday, the 15th.

Helen: Ah yes, that's right, SAA 235 from Johannesburg to Cape Town at 9 am. OK. What would you like to change?

Adam: Would it be possible to fly three days later?

Helen: OK, let me just check the availability. … Ah yes. There are flights on Thursday the 18th, but unfortunately the nine o'clock flight is full. What about another time that day?

Adam: Is it possible to go in the morning? Are there other morning flights?

Helen: There's another flight at 11.30. How about that?

Adam: 11.30 sounds good.

Helen: OK that's great. There's a different flight number. It's SAA 327. Now one thing I just need to sort out with you is that your original ticket was a budget economy class ticket and…

Adam: Yes, that's right.

Helen: Well, it's the cheapest fare and unfortunately that can only be changed if it's upgraded. So you'd need to get a normal economy class ticket.

Adam: Normal economy class? So does that mean I have to pay more for another ticket?

Helen: Yes, you do.

Adam: Oh. How much more do I have to pay?

Helen: Er, let me check … Er that's 740 rand. Is that OK?

Adam: Oh that's quite a bit but … but I'll change it anyway.

Helen: OK. All right. Let me just print this out for you – print out your new itinerary.

🔘63

1 Would it be possible to fly three days later?

2 Is it possible to go in the morning?

🔘64 (Tom = South African)

Adam: I've got a problem. Perhaps you can help me.

Tom: Yes, I'm sure I can. So what's the problem?

Adam: Well, I booked a trip to Cape Point and Peninsula for tomorrow. The problem is that today I did another tour – the Table Mountain tour.

Tom: Right. That's the hike isn't it?

Adam: Yes, and we walked all day and …

Tom: Yes, it's a really good trip.

Adam: But I hurt my leg, so I don't think I can do the tour tomorrow.

Tom: Oh right. That's the one by bike, isn't it?

Adam: Yeah. I really don't want to do more exercise.

Tom: Yeah, I can imagine.

Adam: So I'd like to cancel the booking.

Tom: Hmm. OK, so let me just check on the system. Have you already paid a deposit?

Adam: Oh yes, there was a deposit of 150 rand.

Tom: Unfortunately, if you cancel now, you will lose that deposit.

Adam: Oh. Why is that?

Tom: Well, because the company needs more than 24 hours notice.

Adam: Oh, I see. Oh well …

Tom: You can use the deposit for another activity.

Adam: Yeah?

Tom: We could look at something that doesn't involve exercise.

Adam: Good idea.

Tom: A trip that lots of people do is a boat trip to Robben Island.

Adam: OK.

Tom: Would you be interested in doing that?

Adam: Yeah, that sounds interesting.

65 (Tom = South African)

Tom: Hello. Can I help you?

Tom: That's a pity. Well, you could hire a car for a day.

Tom: Oh dear. Well, you could do a day bus trip.

Unit 10

66

Global warming has made the news again and it's all because of this hot weather we're having. Britain is experiencing a heat wave this summer and it's causing numerous problems. It's difficult to work. It's difficult to sleep. And it's causing health problems too. It's not a little problem. It's serious. 100 people have died in the last few months. The weather is changing. Temperatures above 30 degrees are becoming more common. But it's not just here that temperatures are rising. The rest of Europe is experiencing the hottest summer in 115 years. The weather is getting warmer everywhere and in Antarctica, the ice is melting. Experts say temperatures around the world are rising and we can expect them to continue to rise by about five degrees in the next 100 years. The earth is getting hotter.

And there are other climate changes happening around the world. We've heard about the floods in India and the fires in the United States. In the South Pacific, there were more cyclones this year than last year. And they're getting bigger.

So what's causing all this? Are these changes due to global warming? Are we causing these problems? Some experts say temperatures are rising because we are causing too much pollution. Others say it is part of a natural cycle and we aren't doing anything to cause it. Either way, what can we do about it? These are the topics we'll be discussing on the programme today.

67

a So what's causing all this?

b Are these changes due to global warming?

c Are we causing these problems?

68

a It's difficult to work.

b It's difficult to sleep.

c It's causing health problems.

d In Antarctica, the ice is melting.

e The earth is getting hotter.

f We've heard about the floods in India.

69 (Speaker 2 = Indian; Speaker 3 = American)

Speaker 1:

The trouble with global warming er … everybody thinks any change in the weather is the result of global warming. Occasionally they say, well, yes last year in America they had lots and lots of hurricanes and that's due to global warming. But every 30 years or so they get a lot of hurricanes and it isn't necessarily because of global warming. But the fact there is less ice in the Arctic, that's almost certainly due to global warming. So, I'm not convinced that all our weather problems are because of global warming.

Speaker 2:

Well um global warming, well yeah some people say there is global warming and some say there isn't. I'm not an expert so I don't really know but er, I've um … but I think that we have created a lot of pollution and I think probably … yeah um we probably need to cause less pollution, like not use aeroplanes as often, in order to stop global warming.

Speaker 3:

It seems to me that the weather's changing. Every summer seems to be a bit hotter and we are definitely having more problems with the weather around the world. Um, lots more cyclones and you hear about floods and all sorts of terrible things happening. Yeah I think that's because of global warming. In my opinion, we can do something about it, um, if we try to clean up the environment a bit more, maybe … use public transport more often … and heat our houses with solar energy and that kind of thing. I guess that will make a difference.

70

a Is the weather getting hotter?

b Is global warming a big problem?

c How are people making global warming worse?

d What can we do to stop global warming?

e Should individual people or governments clean up the environment?

Review 1

71

22 I'm having a party on Friday. Do you want to come?

23 Can I buy a discount card from all stations or only from some stations?

24 Did you see the match last night?

25 I have a headache.

26 I have a sore throat.

27 You can go kayaking.

28 It costs $20.

29 I'd like to go surfing.

30 Pollution is getting worse.

CD2 Work and Study

Unit 11

2 (Lilian = Brazilian; Declan = Irish)

Lilian: Nice to meet you, Declan. My name is Lilian Oliveira. And I'm pleased to have you here.

Declan: Thank you. Thanks a million.

Lilian: I'm … I'm in the marketing team – Assistant Manager.

Declan: Oh right. Nice to meet you.

Lilian: Is this your first time in Brazil?

Declan: Yes, so it is, it's amazing.

Lilian: It's the place that never sleeps!

Declan: So I've heard!

Lilian: Well, I have our schedule for today.

Declan: Ah grand.

Lilian: First of all you'll meet my colleague, Teresa Silva.

Declan: Yes.

Lilian: She's the Sales Manager.

Declan: All right.

Lilian: You can talk to her about exporting our coffee to you in Ireland.

Declan: Great. And what time is that?

Lilian: At ten o'clock, in half an hour, Teresa is going to come here. Then she's going to introduce you to Paulo Souza, the Marketing Manager – at quarter to eleven.

Declan: Right.

Lilian: And after that you're having lunch at 12.30 with Fernando.

Declan: Fernando Pinto?

Lilian: Yes, he's our CEO, the Chief Executive Officer. And later on, after lunch, you'll be able to visit the factory. You can look at all the brands that we have and see what you like best. That'll be at 2.15.

Declan: Right. Now, will there be an opportunity to do some tasting?

Lilian: Oh of course! We've organized that for 3pm.

Declan: Fantastic. That's grand, looking forward to that.

Lilian: After the visit you can come back to the hotel.* You'll be back by 4.30 … Relax a little and later on we'll have dinner … at 8 o'clock.

Declan: All right.

Lilian: And we've arranged a visit tomorrow morning to the plantation – if you'd like to go.

Declan: I'd love that. How far away is the plantation?

Lilian: Maybe 400 kilometres from São Paulo.

Declan: Right.

Lilian: But we … the company has hired a helicopter so we'll get there at 11 am.

Declan: I've never been in a helicopter before.

Lilian: Teresa will go with you and you'll be shown around by Victor Gomez, the Plantation Manager. I hope you like it. And I hope you'll buy our coffee.

☞*Did you notice?

Lilian says *You can come back to the hotel.* A native speaker would say *You can go back to the hotel.*

🔊 **3** (Lilian = Brazilian)

What am I doing at 10am?
Who am I meeting at 11.30?
Are there any plans for this afternoon?
What will happen at the end of the day?

🔊 **4**

This is your schedule for the day. First, you're going to talk to the Sales Manager, Paul Johnson, at ten o'clock this morning. Then at half past eleven, you're meeting the Marketing Manager, Sarah Philips. After that, you'll have lunch with the marketing team at half past twelve. This afternoon you'll be able to visit our shop, if you want. I've booked a taxi to the airport at four o'clock this afternoon.

🔊 **5** (Gustavo = Brazilian; Declan = Irish)

Gustavo: What kind of business are you in?

Declan: Now, I own three coffee shops – cafés – a small chain in … in Cork in Ireland and so I've been looking at coffee to get some good quality coffee to import. Now, I went to visit a company called 'Café Perfeito do Brasil'. I've been talking to them and tasting some of their coffee. It's been … it's been wonderful, it has.

Gustavo: Yeah, I know that company – very good coffee. What are you going to do, um, … you want to export to Ireland?*

Declan: Well, I plan to make coffee that is better than some of the big chains with a better quality flavour. Because I often feel those large chains, like … the flavour of the coffee is not good. So, what I've been looking for is high-quality beans to make top-quality coffee and … it seems to be working. Business has been good. I'd like to expand and open up more cafés in other cities in Ireland.

Gustavo: And did you drink good coffee here in Brazil?

Declan: At 'Café Perfeito' I had very good coffee, so I did.

Gustavo: Yes I think you will be very happy with this company.

Declan: I hope so.

Gustavo: You like São Paulo?*

Declan: Yes, but I wasn't expecting it to be such a big city – it's like being in New York! All these high-rise buildings! Yesterday we went on a trip to a coffee plantation by helicopter. It was grand.

☞*Did you notice?

Gustavo says *You want to export to Ireland?* A native speaker would say *Do you want to export to Ireland?*
Gustavo says *You like São Paulo?* A native speaker would say *Do you like São Paulo?*

🔊 **6**

a I plan to make coffee that is better than some of the big chains.

b I'd like to expand and open up more cafés.

Unit 12

🔊 **7** (Francesca = Italian)

Carrie: So, Francesca, we've been working for an hour or so now. Do you want to take a break?

Francesca: Ah, yes please, that would be good.

Carrie: OK. Um. Do you want to talk about what you've done so far?

Francesca: Yeah. Well, I've already filled the sugar bowls.

Carrie: Oh great. So you've done all of them?

Francesca: Yes.

Carrie: Fantastic. What about the knives and forks – have you put those out yet?

Francesca: Ah yeah I've put them out.

Carrie: OK – they're all on the tables?

Francesca: Yeah.

Carrie: Oh perfect. And have you also done the napkins?

Francesca: Um, yes, I've folded them, but I haven't put them out yet.

Carrie: OK. I'll double-check as well … It took me ages to learn to fold them correctly.

Francesca: If it's no good, er tell me and I can do it again.

Carrie: Yeah, no problem. How about the um … water jugs?

Francesca: Ah yeah I've filled the water jugs and put them in the refrigerator.

Carrie: Thanks.

Francesca: But I haven't put the menus on the tables yet. Do I have to put them out?

Carrie: Um, yeah, we should do that before we open.

Francesca: I'll do that later. I've put flowers on every table but I still need to put the salt and pepper out.

Carrie: OK. Um, we also need to put glasses on all the tables. I notice that there aren't glasses on the tables.

Francesca: Oh, sorry, I just … forgot.

Carrie: That's OK. We've still got an hour or so, so you can do that now. I'll check them after you've done it … Um, and maybe right before we open, we should light the candles. But we don't want to do that yet. Maybe just 15 minutes before service time.

Francesca: Sure. I'll do it later.

Carrie: OK … OK. Do you have any other questions?

Francesca: Do you want me to cut the bread as well?

Carrie: Oh yes please. See you later then.

🔊 **8** (Francesca = Italian)

Carrie: OK, well, that's it. They were the last customers, so we're done for the evening. So, how did you find it? How did it go?

Francesca: I enjoyed it.

Carrie: Oh good – good. Oh that's really nice 'cos I think it went really well overall and you're very friendly and natural with the customers.

Francesca: Thank you.

Carrie: Umm … Well, there are just a few little things …

Francesca: Sure.

Carrie: Um, I noticed that the food – the plates … sort of stayed on the table for a few minutes after the people were finished. But usually what we like to do is, once both people or everyone at the table has finished, can you just make sure you clear the plates as soon as possible?

Francesca: OK … OK.

Carrie: Yeah, this way they can have a bit of space and have some time to just chat a bit and if they want dessert and … yeah.

Francesca: OK, I'll make sure I do it next time.

Carrie: No, it's not a big deal, like I said it was just a little thing.

Francesca: Oh yeah.

Carrie: And just one more thing. Um, it'd be really good if you could just try to keep the water glasses filled. Just fill them if you notice that they're empty as you're walking around or when you're taking orders.

Francesca: Oh OK, I thought if I do that, probably I'll just interrupt them.

Carrie: Oh good point – good point. No, it's fine if you can just very quietly go over and fill them.

Francesca: Oh OK I'll do that. Thank you very much for the advice.

Carrie: Um how about tips – how did you do?

Francesca: Um, I got about £35.

Carrie: £35? That's pretty good. Actually that's really good for your first night. Most people only make about £15.

Francesca: Really?

Carrie: Yeah, yeah. Like I said, I think you're a natural and sometimes on your first night you make a bit less, but that's actually really good. But you work for it, don't you? Do you have any questions or anything you want to talk about?

Francesca: Not really … I enjoyed working here.

Carrie: Yeah. Like I said, you did really well. And it gets easier as you go on. The first night's always the most difficult one.

Francesca: Thank you.

● 9

the plates as soon as possible
There are just a few

● 10 (Sergei = Russian)

Sergei: Oh right.

Sergei: Yes sure.

Sergei: Sure. Anything else?

Sergei: OK.

Unit 13

● 11 (Brad = Australian)

Hi Raman. It's Brad here. Look, I'm afraid I won't be in today. My son is a bit crook and he's off school so I have to stay home to look after him. I'm really sorry to leave this message for you, but I've got to take my son to the doctor. Er, do you remember the training session next week? You know, the one about the new computer system? I've organized the trainer so there's no need to contact him and I've booked the room, but there are a few other things that need doing. I need you to organize the projector that goes with the laptop, er, you can do that with reception. And you'll need to sort out lunch for about ten people. Yes, that's right – there'll be ten of us. Talk to Alison at reception – she'll know some good cafés we can order from. Oh and stationery! Yes, I need you to make sure that everyone has a notepad and a pen and one of those … er what do you call them? Er sorry, I'm not thinking very clearly this morning … you know, one of those really big things, like a pad of paper for writing up notes … er flip charts – that's what we call them. Yeah, um a flip chart would be really useful – one is enough, er, with some marker pens to write on it. Really, really sorry to leave all these instructions for you on a phone message, Raman, but I'm sure you'll know what to do. Er, might call you back this arvo and see how you've got on. Bye for now.

● 12 (Raman = Indian; Alison = Australian)

Raman: Hello Alison.

Alison: G'day Raman.

Raman: You know how Brad has asked me to order lunch for our training session next week?

Alison: Yeah. How's it going?

Raman: Well, I have two prices for the lunch and I'm not sure which one to choose.

Alison: OK.

Raman: So the first one is from The Tasman Café. It's more expensive. $300 just for the food. And the delivery is an extra $10, but I could go and get it myself.

Alison: They're just in the High Street, aren't they?

Raman: That's right. And the other price is from The Lunch Box. Do you know them?

Alison: They're a bit further out of town, aren't they, in the shopping mall? They're quite good.

Raman: OK. So which café do people normally use?

Alison: Well, it sort of depends on who is coming to the lunch. This is just for the training, isn't it?

Raman: Yes, it is.

Alison: Right. OK. Well, I'd probably use The Lunch Box then.

Raman: All right. Why?

Alison: Um, I mean, if the lunch is for managers, then you'll probably use The Tasman Café.

Raman: Well, The Lunch Box is $250, so it's definitely cheaper.

Alison: I mean, the food from The Tasman Cafe is probably nicer. What's the difference in the type of food?

Raman: Well, The Tasman Café has gourmet sandwiches, not just ordinary sandwiches. So, you know, the food will probably taste better from the Tasman Café. And also you get sushi. You get much more variety. But The Lunch Box is cheaper. Mind you, with The Lunch Box we have to pay delivery and that's $20. Their delivery charge is more expensive. So that makes it a total of $270.

Alison: What's the total for The Tasman Café then?

Raman: Well, if I go and pick up the lunch, it's $300. So it's only a difference of $30.

Alison: That's not bad. It's much nicer food – for the money.

Raman: Let's order from The Tasman Café then.

Alison: Yeah – beaut!

● 13

The Tasman Café has gourmet sandwiches, not just ordinary sandwiches.

● 14

a   There's vegetarian sushi, not just ordinary sushi.

b   We can get hot savouries, not just cold savouries.

c   They have chocolate cake, not just orange cake.

d   They sell fresh coffee, not just instant coffee.

● 15 (Raman = Indian; Colleague = Australian)

Raman: Hi there. I'm ordering food for the conference. Can I ask you some questions?

Colleague: Yes, of course.

Raman: Do you prefer hot or cold food?

Colleague: I think cold food is easier.

Raman: OK, and what about drinks – do you prefer hot or cold?

Colleague: Hot drinks are better.

Raman: I'm trying to decide between a buffet or a sit-down meal. What do you think?

Colleague: A buffet is more convenient.

Raman: And should I order fruit or cake for dessert?

Colleague: I think fruit is healthier.

● 16 (Raman = Indian)

Raman: Hi there. I'm ordering food for the conference. Can I ask you some questions?

Raman: Do you prefer hot or cold food?

Raman: OK, and what about drinks – do you prefer hot or cold?

Raman: I'm trying to decide between a buffet or a sit-down meal. What do you think?

Raman: And should I order fruit or cake for dessert?

Unit 14

🔘 17 (Paul Dugan = American)

Good morning everyone. Today I'm going to talk to you about how to manage money. I'm afraid I'm not going to tell you how to get rich quick, but I will tell you some simple things you can do that will help you save more money. So, I'm going to give you five tips … simple but important advice to make sure you manage your money successfully.

Now the first point, and perhaps the most important one, is about how much you spend. It's really important that you don't overspend. For example, if you earn $2000 a month, don't spend $2500. This is really simple. You have a problem if you spend more money than you earn. Spending less doesn't have to be difficult. You can just cut back or reduce what you spend by a little, just a few small things … then it can make a big saving. Maybe just buy one cup of coffee a day, instead of two. These small changes can make a difference.

Ah, the next point is about how much you earn. It's important that your salary is appropriate for your job. It's OK if your employer pays you too much, but make sure he or she doesn't pay you too little. Find out how your salary compares to other people doing the same kind of job in two or three other companies. If you're going to work long hours or have lots of responsibility, you need to make sure you're getting paid enough.

Er, another important point is that you need a budget. That's a simple plan of what you spend your money on. If you have a plan, it will make saving money a lot easier. Everyone needs a budget. It doesn't matter how much money you earn … I can't stress this enough. Make sure you have a budget! And make sure you use it. Don't just write it and forget about it.

🔘 18 (Paul Dugan = American)

OK, now my fourth point is about managing your debt. Before you borrow money, think about what you are borrowing it for. It's a good idea to borrow money to buy assets, for example, to buy a house. And it's a good idea to pay for your education. These things will still be worth something when you have finished paying off the debt. It isn't a good idea to borrow money for non-essentials, for example, expensive clothes, holidays or dinner at a nice restaurant. It's easy to use your credit card for these things, but your credit card can get you into trouble if you don't use it properly. If you use credit cards, and I don't recommend it, it's important you know how much you are spending on them. Then, when the bill comes, pay the total bill every month. Don't just pay the minimum amount, don't just pay a little every month, don't just pay 20 dollars a month because you will always pay more. You are paying the interest, what the credit card company adds on in interest. So at the end of the day, that watch you bought for 100 dollars, if you pay it off slowly, that watch is going to cost you double that.

And my final tip for managing your money is to plan your savings. It's a good idea to save about ten per cent of your salary every month. Include this saving in your budget and try and increase how much you save every year. You could do this by increasing what you earn or decreasing what you spend, or both! Try and focus on saving money, not just paying the bills. It's another way of looking at things and it's a lot more positive. So, there are five tips for managing your money successfully. They are simple but they work.

Unit 15

🔘 19

So, welcome to English Studies International everyone … welcome to the school. My name is Anna and I'm the Director of Studies.

All right, so the first thing is what's happening today? So from 9 am until 10.30, you'll do some tests. You'll have a written test that tests your grammar and your vocabulary, OK? You will also do a self-assessment. Self-assessment is – you think about your level. You think about your speaking, your writing, your reading, your listening and you decide your level. Now, it doesn't matter in what order you do the written test and the self-assessment. You can either do the test first or you can do the self-assessment first. You will also have an interview – that's speaking – a speaking assessment. So you'll have a written test, a self-assessment and an interview. These three help us decide your level. All right, so that's from nine and then … umm … after you've done the tests, at about half past ten, you can have a break.

After the break at about 10.45, Rebecca will be waiting for you in reception to give you your books.

At eleven o'clock, please come back here to the Learning Centre, and Stewart, the Manager, will give you an introduction to the Learning Centre. At half past eleven you will meet Christine. Christine will talk to you about the social programme at English Studies International. These are all the activities that you can do after school. So that's until midday. Then at midday, I will come back. You will meet me again and I'll give you your timetables – your personal timetables that will tell you your class and your teacher and the rooms. Then you can have lunch in the canteen. During lunch, Berit will be in her office if any of you have accommodation problems. Then, this afternoon you could either listen to a talk about London or you could do a conversation class if you know London already. You will start your normal classes tomorrow morning.

🔘 20

Before we begin the first activity I'd … um … I'd just like to talk about a few classroom rules. You know, to help your learning. These are rules for all my students. OK, so, the first one – the most important rule – when you're in here, inside the classroom, you must speak English. You all have lots of different first languages so it makes sense to use English to talk to each other. So we've got two Italian speakers here – when you're in class, you must speak only in English. OK? It's a really good way of getting more speaking practice. A second rule is about being on time in the morning. Lessons start at nine o'clock so you must get here on time – before nine is even better – so we can all start studying together. It's not really very polite to arrive 20 minutes late because it disturbs the people who did come on time. It makes things hard for your classmates. And another thing – mobile phones. You mustn't use your mobile during the lesson. Again, it's not very polite. In fact, please turn your phone off completely during the lesson.

21 (Bruno = Spanish; Mei Lin = Chinese)

Mei Lin: What was your first lesson like?

Bruno: It was fun – we did a lot of speaking.

Mei Lin: Just speaking?

Bruno: More or less – getting to know the other students. And our teacher talked about some rules in the classroom.

Mei Lin: What kind of rules?

Bruno: Well, we have to speak English all the time and we have to try to be on time in the morning.

Mei Lin: That'll be difficult for you!

Bruno: Yeah, but it is OK to arrive 20 minutes late.

Mei Lin: 20 minutes?

Bruno: Yeah. Oh, and we aren't allowed to have our mobile phones on.

22

You have to speak English in class.

23

a   You have to speak English in class.
b   You have to arrive on time.
c   You have to turn your mobile phone off.

24

a   --
Toby: At nine o'clock.
b   --
Toby: Of course. You can wait in the classroom.
c   --
Toby: I'll give you some most nights.
d   --
Toby: Yes, you do. We'll use it in class all the time.
e   --
Toby: Yes, of course you are.

Unit16

25 (Mayuki = Japanese)

Nigel: So what are you doing outside class to improve your English?

Mayuki: Ah. Speaking. I try to speak a lot. I talk English with Japanese friends. Only English.

Nigel: Oh cool. That's really good because sometimes it's really hard to speak English to people who speak the same language as you.

Mayuki: Yes. Erm … it's difficult to speak English.

Nigel: Mmm. Don't worry if you make mistakes when you're talking. It's

important people understand you, and a few little mistakes often don't matter.

Mayuki: OK. I want … it is not easy to speak English. First I think in Japanese and translate to English.

Nigel: It will get easier. Just keep practising your speaking a lot. OK?

Mayuki: OK … but um … I want to study listening this week. I want to watch DVD.*

Nigel: I think it's important to watch DVDs in English. Do you do that?

Mayuki: Yes. I like to. When I watch DVD* I can listen to English, natural English and vocabulary and pronunciation.

Nigel: So when you watch DVDs … um, what do you do? Do you use the subtitles or … how do you do it?

Mayuki: Of course I use subtitles!

Nigel: And do you watch all of the movie?

Mayuki: Yes.

Nigel: OK. What some students find really useful is to watch part of a movie. But you could watch this part three or four times. Just watch maybe five or ten minutes. And so you're not watching the whole thing, just, um, a short section. And the first time why not listen for general meaning only? Don't try and understand everything. And the second time, the second time listen and try to understand more detail, what each person's saying. And then, the third time, turn the subtitles on. OK, so the first two times watch it without subtitles. OK? So then you'll be listening really carefully. Um, and then after that you could listen again a fourth time and focus on vocabulary or pronunciation. So rather than watching the whole thing … it's still useful but … actually focus on a short section and watch it again and again and focus on different things each time. Does that sound useful?

Mayuki: Yes it does. I'll try that.

☞*Did you notice?

Mayuki says: *I want to watch DVD.* A native speaker would say: *I want to watch a DVD* or *I want to watch DVDs.* She makes the same mistake when she says: *When I watch DVD I can listen to English…* A native speaker would say: *When I watch a DVD I can listen to English* or *When I watch DVDs I can listen to English.*

26 (Mayuki = Japanese)

Nigel: OK Mayuki, here's an advice sheet that will help you. First you need to set some goals, um, you need to think about what you need to do in English. You've said that speaking and listening

are important for you, so think, um, in a bit more detail about what kinds of speaking and listening are important for you. So, er … for speaking, for example, you know, do you need to talk on the telephone or in everyday conversations? And for listening, what sort of things do you want to listen to? The news, seminars, erm presentations? So think about your speaking and listening in more detail. Ah so for you … what are your goals?

Mayuki: Hmm … My main goal is to talk to foreign visitors easily when they visit our company. I need to talk about my job. Ah … I also want to talk to people when I go overseas on holiday.

Nigel: OK, good. Next you need to find things to help you reach your goals. Find material. Use listening and speaking books in the self-access centre, er conversation groups, friends … lots of things help. I'll show you some things later.

Mayuki: OK.

Nigel: And then, once you're studying, once you're actually using those things, er, … you need to … to stop and think about your learning. Ask yourself questions about what you've done. Er, what did you learn? Maybe you learned a lot or maybe you didn't learn anything new. How useful was it? If it was useful, then you will probably use it again. Do you need to change anything? If it wasn't useful, you need to decide if you will do things differently next time. You might want to make it a little bit easier next time or more interesting. You need to stop and think about what you studied. OK?

Mayuki: Mmm, OK.

Nigel: If you do this, it will make your learning a lot better and a lot easier.

Review2

19   It's a thing for going online, you know, a small computer.
20   The café has chocolate cake but the shop only has fruit cake.
21   What's your schedule for today?
22   What are your learning goals?

Answerkey

Unit 1

Get ready to listen and speak
○ *Your own answers.*
○ *Your own answers.*

A
1 c They talk about what Brian did last weekend but most of the conversation is about Mark's birthday party.
2 and 3 Mark called last night. It's his birthday ~~this~~ *next* week and he's having a party on ~~Friday~~ *Saturday* to celebrate. It starts at ~~eight o'clock~~ *7.30*. ~~He wants me to take some food.~~ *He doesn't want me to take anything.* I'm looking forward to it.

B
1 No. Mark asks how Brian is and he also asks about his weekend.
2 2e 3f 4b 5d 6a
3 c
4, 5 and 6

Invitation	Reply to invitation
I was wondering if you wanted to come. (1) Do you want to come? (3) Would you like to come? (2)	That sounds good. That'd be nice. I'd love to.

7 I'm afraid I'm going away at the weekend.
I work on Saturday evenings.

Sound smart
1 /t/   2 a

Focus on beginning and ending phone conversations
Beginning: a and c   End: b, d and e

8 *Possible answers:*
Hi Mark, how are you?
Fine, thanks.
Yes, lovely. What about you?
That sounds good. What day?
What time?
Do you want me to bring anything?
Great.
Bye.
9 *Possible answers:*
Fine. How are you?
Have you had a good weekend?
Not too bad. Actually the reason I'm ringing is because it's my birthday next week and I'm having a party. Would you like to come?
Friday night.
Eight o'clock.
No, I'll have food and everything.
See you on Friday. Bye.

C
1 b
2 1 a He says 'a few more people have just arrived so I'd better go and say hi'.
2 c Reshma says 'I live next door'.
3 c Reshma says 'I've known him since he moved in, a couple of years ago'. 'A couple' means 'about two'.

D
1 Conversation A: jobs. Conversation B: weather.
2 a So what do you do?, It's cold today, isn't it?
b What do you do there?, Do you like it?, What about you?, What do you do?, Do you think it'll snow?

Focus on questions to start conversations
b It's nice food, isn't it?
c They look good, don't they?
d She's from Taiwan, isn't she?
e He doesn't look happy, does he?

3 *Your own answers. Possible answers:*
Jobs: What do you do? How long have you worked there?
Weather: It's rained a lot today, hasn't it? Did you get wet coming here?
Where you are: Do you know anyone here? How long have you known him / her?
People's interests: Have you seen any good films recently? Who was in it?
4 *Your own answers.*

Unit 2

Get ready to listen and speak
○ 1B 2C 3A
○ *Your own answers.*

A
1 A
2 b Arawa c 10 d 5 e No. One of the bedrooms is a double bedroom but the other bedroom only fits a single bed in it.   f No. There is a small area where you can hang your washing but no garden.   g 5.30.

B
1 Susan says 'Sorry, thirty six …' She repeats part of the answer and waits for the other speaker to finish it. She doesn't ask a question.
2 b It stays the same. This shows she hasn't finished what she wants to say. When you finish what you want to say, your intonation should go down, so the other speaker knows they can speak.
3 It rises (↗) to show Susan is asking a question.
4 b Sorry, it's a ten-minute walk to …
c Sorry, you'll be down there at …

Focus on asking questions

1 a 'I was just wondering …' is more polite.
2 In a the word order is the same as in statements: subject + verb.
   In b the word order is the same as in questions: verb + subject.
3 b I was just wondering how much it is.
   c I was just wondering how many bedrooms there are.
   d I was just wondering when I can move in.

Sound smart

1 I was just wondering <u>where</u> it is.

C

1 The oven is broken. Susan says 'the oven's not working'.
2 a last night b Yes, she checked the plug. c He will try and fix the oven. If he can't, he will call an electrician. d 7 pm tomorrow

D

1 2 a 3 d 4 c
2 <u>there's a broken window. We can't close it</u> (send someone around to fix it?)
3 *Your own answers.*
4 *Your own answers.*

Unit3

Get ready to listen and speak

○ *Your own answers.*
○ *Your own answers.*

A

1 b and d
2 b 50 c 1000 d 5000 e map
3 a True b True c False. You put it in a machine.

Focus on saying numbers

1 b   2 a   3 b   4 a

B

1 Understanding: b. Actions: d
2 b How will I know the correct ticket price? c Then what do I do? d What should I do next? e How can I tell if a machine takes credit cards?

C

1 b and c
2 No-My-Car-Day Card: c d f g   Rainbow Card: b e f

D

1 or. No, you don't need to repeat the verb because it is the same.

Sound smart

1
Do I get this discount pass from <u>normal</u> ticket machines or from <u>special</u> ticket machines?

2 b Do I buy a discount card from all stations or only some stations?
   c Do I buy a Rainbow Card only on Monday or any day?
   d Do I buy a 500 yen card or 1000 yen card?
   e Do I get a discount of 200 yen or 250 yen?
   f Do I use a Rainbow Card at the usual ticket gate or at a special ticket gate?
3 *Possible answers*:
   b Can I use 10,000 yen notes?
   c How will I know which notes I can use?
   d Can I buy a discount ticket?
   e Do I buy one every Friday or only on some Fridays?

Unit4

Get ready to listen and speak

○ *Your own answers.*

A

1 (Cambodian) Thai ✓ Indian ✓ Vietnamese ✓
2 and 3 *Possible answers*:
   b Rachel says that she is 'getting a bit bored with Thai'. This means she has probably eaten Thai food recently.
   c It's on Queen Street.
   d No, it's not as strong as Thai food.
   e It's reasonable. It's not cheap but not too expensive.

B

1 b No, a, c and e are followed by the infinitive.

Sound smart

1 They are all b.
   Rising intonation. Shows that you are enthusiastic about your suggestion. If your intonation does not go up a lot, you can make the idea sound boring.

2 b Let's have salad for dinner.
   c How about going to a Chinese restaurant for dinner?
   d We could have pizza for dinner.
   e Let's go to a Turkish restaurant for dinner.
   f Shall we eat sushi for dinner?
   g How about having roast chicken for dinner?
   h We could try a Mexican restaurant for dinner.

C

1 chicken 2   noodles ✗   lime leaves 1   mushroom soup 1
   egg ✗   chicken curry parcel 2   curry 2   beef ✗
   fish sauce 2   ginger 2   tomatoes ✗   lemongrass 1
   coriander ✗   coconut milk 2   mushrooms 1   rice 2
2 I went to the Khmer Café for dinner on Friday. For a starter, I had shrimp ~~curry~~ *soup*. There was a taste of coconut and lime. It was quite ~~sweet~~ *salty*. Then for a main course I had ~~vegetable~~ *beef* stir-fry. It's made with pineapple and tomatoes. This dish was very ~~mild~~ *spicy*. For a dessert I had fried bananas and ~~honey~~ *ice cream*. It was ~~OK~~ *delicious*.

Answer key

D

1 Neil: c d b a
Rachel: c d a b

2 We don't use *course* with *starter* and *dessert*. You can say *a dessert* or *dessert*.

3 b Last night I went to a Japanese restaurant. For a starter, I had miso soup. It was tasty. It's made with tofu and onion.
c Last night I went to a Spanish restaurant. For a main course I had paella. It was full of flavour. It's made with seafood and rice.
d Last night I went to a Chinese restaurant. For a main course I had beef stir-fry. It was quite spicy. It's made with broccoli and ginger.
e Last night I went to a French restaurant. For dessert, I had crème brulée. It was really sweet. It's made with vanilla and cream.
f Last night I went to a Turkish restaurant. For a main course I had shish kebab. It was delicious. It's made with lamb and peppers.

4 *Your own answers.*

Unit5

Get ready to listen and speak
- *Your own answers.*
- *Your own answers.*

A

1 Arnaud went to a football game and lost his camera on the bus.

2 b F He lost it on the bus.   c F He telephoned the bus company.
d T   e T   f T   g F They will go to the police in ten minutes.

B

1 a No I didn't.
b Are you?

2 b and d

3 and 4
b Did you?   c I didn't.   d it   e I haven't   f I'd like to.

5 *Possible answers:*
a Great (not 'It was great').
b *Star Wars* (not 'I saw *Star Wars*').
c Really good.
d Last summer (not 'I went last summer').
e My family (not 'I went with my family')
f Yes, I did.

Sound smart
1 b What did you do?
c Did you go to the cinema?
d What did you see?
e Did you like the film?
f Did you go with friends?
2 I <u>did.</u>
I <u>didn't</u>.

C

1 and 2
b 27 Park Road
c B13 4TY
d 07901 672301
e arnaudl1@hotmail.com
f on the number 16 bus
g 11am Saturday
h digital
i case
j old

D

1 a Can you describe the camera to me please?
b What's it like?
c Do you know what make it is?

2

Size	Colour	Age	Brand	Type	Other
		not very old	Nikon		shoulder strap, grey case, name inside

3

Size	Colour	Age	Brand	Type	Other
big	silver brown red black	3 years old quite old new	Nokia Gucci	sports woman's	hard case black handles

4 *Possible answers:*
b They are Gucci sunglasses. They're brown. They have a hard case.
c It's a big red sports bag. It's quite old and it has black handles.
d It's a Nokia mobile phone. It's small and black.

5 *Your own answers.*

Unit6

Get ready to listen and speak
- 2 f 3 a 4 b 5 c 6 e 7 g

A

1 a a cough   b headache   c sore eyes

2 b two   c two   d 24   e eight   f one or two   g twice

B

1 and 2
What to do: You need to take, You must take, You should take, Take.
What not to do: You mustn't take, You shouldn't take.

Sound smart
1 You should <u>take</u> paracetamol.
<u>Don't</u> take it when you cough.
You <u>shouldn't</u> take it for longer than that.
You <u>mustn't</u> take more than that.
2 The main verb (take) is stressed in positive sentences. The negative (don't, shouldn't, mustn't) is stressed in negative sentences.

3 sore throat – lozenges
swollen knee – ice
sore eyes – drops
cough – cough mixture

4 *Possible answers:*

b   Oh no. You need to take some lozenges. They will help.

c   Oh no. You should put ice on it. It will help.

d   Oh no. Don't use the computer and put some drops in your eyes. They will help.

e   Oh no. You should take some painkillers. They will help.

f   Oh no. You should take some cough mixture. It will help.

C

1   2 c   3 d   4 a   5 e

2   Ali: lemon   Seiji: Chinese radish, honey   Ana: garlic

3   b   hot   c   lemon   d   sore throat   e   carrot   f   juice
g   drink   h   water   i   half hour   j   two   k   three

D

1   kind   b   which   c   like

2   Yes

3

A	B
hot lemon juice	drink
mandarins	small orange
vapour rub	cream

4   *Possible answers:*

You should make hot lemon juice, which is a drink.

You should eat mandarins. They're a kind of small orange.

You should use vapour rub. It's a bit like a cream.

5   *Your own answers.*

Unit 7

Get ready to listen and speak

○   2 d   3 a   4 b

○   *Possible answers:*

cheapest ← → most expensive

campsite   hostel   guesthouse   hotel

A

1   guesthouse, hotel and hostel.

2

Place	Price ($)	Share room	Share bathroom	Breakfast
The Vancouver Inn	110	✗	✗	✓
BC Lodge	30	✓	✓	✓
The Maple Leaf Villa	60	✗	✓	?

B

1   Making a general enquiry: b
Asking for more detailed information: d   g
Saying 'no': c   e
Showing interest: f   h

2   a   It's too far from the centre.   b   I'm not keen on cooking my own breakfast.   c   That sounds really good.   d   It's too far from the airport.   e   I'm not keen on sleeping in a tent.   f   That sounds great.

1   first syllable

2   noisy   quiet   hotel   central   luggage   private   hostel
'Hotel' is stressed on the second syllable, but the other words are all stressed on the first syllable.

3   expensive   convenient   interesting   possible

3 and 4   *Possible answers:*

b   I'm looking for somewhere central.   c   It's too far from the centre.   d   I'm not keen on staying somewhere noisy.   e   That sounds good.

C

1   Room 2 kitchen   Room 3 bedroom   Room 4 bathroom

2

Room	Feature
2	microwave, fridge
3	big bed, sink, desk, comfortable chair
4	power shower, plenty of towels

3   a   30   b   No, but you can if you want to   c $60   d   two

Focus on adverbs used with adjectives

They come before an adjective and make it weaker or stronger.

D

1   a   This is the … If you are showing more than one thing, you say *these are*.

b   has got

c   as you can see

2   *Possible answers:*

b   This is my computer. It's got a big screen. As you can see, it's quite new.

c   This is my car. It's got a small engine. As you can see, it's really easy to park.

d   This is my MP3 player. It's got 20 Gb of memory. As you can see, it's very light to carry around.

e   This is my digital camera. It's got a zoom lens. As you can see, it's fairly easy to carry in my pocket.

f   This is my widescreen TV. It's got surround sound. As you can see, it's almost like being at the movies.

Unit 8

Get ready to listen and speak

○   *Your own answers.*

A

1   see dolphins and whales   go bungy jumping
go skydiving   visit an aquarium

2   b   11   c   40   d   bungy jumping   e   45   f   85   g   skydiving
h   3,000   i   6   j 16

Answer key

B

1 oh all right, oh wow.
2 yeah, sounds good, ok, great.
3 *Possible answers:*
   b oh ok c ah ha d oh all right e yeah
   f oh wow (*wow* is used when you are surprised)
4 *Your own answers.*

C

1 b
2 b 1 c Calum Brodie d YES e 200 f Friday g 28 March

D

1 a sentence B b sentence B c would

2 *Your own answers.*
3 *Possible answers:*
   b On Saturday. c Three. d It's Mario Carinci.
   e C-A-R-I-N-C-I f 0056 478 34561

Unit 9

A

1 b
2 b Lister c Monday 15th d SAA 235 e 9 am
   f budget economy g Thursday 18th h 11.30 am
   i normal economy j 740

B

1 1 Would it be / Is it possible to fly tomorrow?
   2 Could I fly tomorrow?
   3 Can I fly tomorrow?
   Note: Number 3 is more direct than the other examples, but it is
   still polite.

2 a Is it possible to travel a week later?
   b Would it be possible to get a refund?
   c Could I change my hotel booking too?
   d Is it possible to leave the following day?
   e Can I buy travel insurance?
   f Would it be possible to organize transport to the hotel?
   g Could I take an earlier flight?
   h Can I get a special meal on the flight?

C

1 a Table Mountain. b Cape Point and Peninsula.
   c Robben Island.
2 b walked c leg d 150 rand e 24 hours f boat

D

1 so
   because
2 I've got (really bad sunburn) so I can't come to the beach.
   I can't come to the beach because I've got really bad sunburn.
3 c I'm afraid of flying so I can't travel by plane.
   d I can't go on the boat trip because I get seasick very easily.
   e I've got a special ticket so I can't change my flight.
   f I haven't got enough money so I can't come to the restaurant
     with you.
   g I can't go hiking because I haven't got the right shoes.
   h I haven't got a driver's licence so I can't hire a car.

4 *Possible answers:*
   I have a problem with a booking. I'm not feeling well so I can't go
   hiking.
   I can't hire a car because I didn't bring my driver's licence with me.
   OK. That's a good idea.

Unit 10

A

1 heatwave, flood, cyclone
2 b health c died d common e 115 f 100 g Floods
   h cyclones i pollution

B

1 Present continuous
2 Fewer: floods aeroplanes fires
   Less: ice pollution rain energy

3 *Possible answers:*

  b Summer is getting longer.

  c Winter is getting warmer.

  d Summer is starting earlier.

  e There is more rain in the winter.

  f There are fewer storms in the summer.

4 and 5 *Your own answers.*

C

1 *Possible answers*: pollution, hotter, weather, aeroplanes.

2 *Your own answers.*

3 a Speaker 1   b Speakers 2 and 3   c Speaker 1

  d Speakers 1 and 3

4 a less ice in the Arctic.

  b *Possible answers:*

    not use aeroplanes as often

    use public transport more often

    heat our houses with solar energy

D

1 b I'm not an expert but … I think   c   It seems to me

  d I think   e In my opinion   f I guess

  I'm not convinced … (You can also say 'I'm not sure (that)' …)

  means the speaker doesn't believe something

  I'm not an expert but … means the speaker doesn't have any

  special knowledge

2 *Possible answers*:

  b I'm not an expert but I think it is a very big problem.

  c I think we cause a lot of pollution by using cars and aeroplanes

    too much.

  d I guess we could use public transport more often.

  e It seems to me that governments have to do more to help.

3 *Your own answers.*

Review 1

Section 1

1 b	4 b	7 a	10 b	13 b
2 c	5 c	8 b	11 a	
3 b	6 b	9 c	12 c	

Section 2

14 jobs, weather, where you are, people's interests.

15 I'm phoning to tell you that the shower's broken. Would it be

  possible to get someone to fix it?

16 The type of missing word, e.g. is it a word or a number? Is it an

  adjective or a noun?

17 Shall we go to a Thai restaurant for dinner?

18 Last night I went to an Italian restaurant. For dessert I had

  tiramisu. It was delicious. It's made with coffee and cream.

19 It's a kind of fruit.

20 I can't travel because I forgot my ticket.

21 I didn't bring my swimming costume so I can't go swimming.

Section 3

22 b

23 'Can I buy a <u>discount</u> card from <u>all</u> stations or only from <u>some</u>

  stations?'

24 b

25–28 *Possible answers*

25 Oh no! Take some painkillers. They will help.

26 Oh no! You should take some lozenges. They will help.

27 Oh wow! Sounds good.

28 Ah ha, yeah.

29 I'd like(to)go surfing.

30 b

Unit 11

Get ready to listen and speak

○ *Your own answers.*

○ True, False (It comes from Arabic), True.

A

1 b Sales Manager   c Marketing Manager   d CEO

  e Plantation Manager

2 and 3

Order	Activity	What time?
3	Have lunch with the CEO.	12.30pm
2	Meet the Marketing Manager.	10.45am
4	Visit the factory.	2.15pm
1	Talk to the Sales Manager.	10am
6	Relax in the hotel before dinner.	4.30pm
7	Visit a coffee plantation by helicopter.	11am tomorrow
5	Taste different coffee.	3pm

B

1 going to introduce   you're having   you'll be able to

2 *Possible answers:*

  1 You're going to talk to the Sales Manager.

  2 You're meeting the Marketing Manager, Sarah Philips.

  3 Yes, you'll be able to visit the shop, if you want.

  4 You're going by taxi to the airport at 4pm.

3 and 4 *Your own answers.*

5 I have your schedule for the afternoon. First, you'll meet our Office

  Manager, Debbie Fulton at two o'clock, then you'll be able to talk

  to our office staff at two thirty, if you want. At three o'clock you're

  having afternoon tea with Debbie and our Customer Services

  Manager, Sam Harris. Next at half past three you're going to

  meet our Company Director, Suzanne Allen. I've arranged hotel

  accommodation for tonight at The Regent Hotel.

C

1 a

2 a three.

  b wonderful.

  c The flavour of the coffee isn't very good.

  d Expand his business and open more cafés.

  e It's bigger than he expected (and has lots of high-rise

    buildings).

3 a plan to make / better than / the big

  b like to / and open / more

Answer key

D

1 *I intend to … is strongest.*

2 b I'd like to hire an assistant.
   c I plan to sell more products online.
   d I hope to employ more staff.
   e I want to close one of our factories.
   f I'd like to increase our profits.
   g I intend to export more products.
   h I plan to do more marketing abroad.
3 *Your own answers.*

Unit 12

A

1 b d g
2 napkins and glasses

B

1 We use *already* in positive sentences.
   We use *yet* in negative sentences and questions.
   Yet comes at the end of a sentence.
2 c I've already arranged the flowers.
   d I haven't checked the reservations list yet.
   e I've already talked to the chef about the menu.
   f I've already put the knives and forks on the tables.
   g I haven't turned on the music yet.
   h I haven't written the menu on the board yet.
   i I've already cut the bread.
   j I haven't lit the candles yet.
3 b Have you checked the till yet?
   c Have you turned on the computer yet?
   d Have you swept the floor yet?
   e Have you unlocked the door yet?

C

1 1 b 2 a 3 b
2 b friendly, natural c clear plates d water glasses e tips

D

1 b ✗ c ✗ d ✓ e ✗ f ✓
2 *Just* makes the feedback less negative.

3 *Possible answers:*
   You: You did well tonight. There are just a few things …
   You: Could you just try to get the meals out as soon as possible?
   You: And can you just make sure you change the napkins after
        each course?
   You: Yes, could you just clear the plates quickly?
4 *Possible answers:*
   a Could you just make sure you smile at the customers as they
      arrive?
   b I think you're a very good waiter.
   c Can you just check that you give customers the correct
      glasses?
   d That was an excellent first night.
   e It'd be really good if you could just bring the bill more quickly.

Unit 13

A

1 projector, laptop, notepad, flipchart, marker pen
2 b The training session is ~~today~~. next week
   c ~~book the room~~. The room is already booked.
   d talk to ~~trainer~~ about the projector. reception
   e arrange lunch for ~~15~~ people. 10
   f give everyone a ~~folder~~ and a pen. notepad
   g get ~~several~~ flipcharts. a

B

1 Brad is direct.
   No, it is not a good idea. Brad is the manager so he uses direct
   language with the people who work for him.
2 Could you … Would you be able to … Do you think you could …
3 *Possible answers:*
   b Could you buy some pens?
   c You'll need to order some flowers.
   d Do you think you could send an e-mail?
   e Would you be able to book a hotel room?
   f You'll need to organize morning tea.
   g Could you get a laptop?

4 (The correct name of the object is given at the end of each
   expression).
   Possible answers:
   b a thing for attaching pieces of paper *(stapler)*
   c a plastic thing full of ink you put in a printer *(printer cartridge)*
   d some white stuff for correcting mistakes *(correction fluid)*
   e a thing for making small holes in paper so you can put the
      paper in a folder *(hole punch)*
   f some stuff for sticking paper together *(glue)*
   g some stuff for cleaning a whiteboard *(whiteboard cleaner)*

C

1 c

2

	The Tasman Café	The Lunch Box
Where café is	near High Street	in the shopping mall
Type of food	sushi	
Total price	$300 ($310 with delivery)	$270

D

1 not just, better, more variery, cheaper, more expensive

Sound smart

1 <u>gourmet</u>
   <u>ordinary</u>

2 and 3 *Possible answers:*
   Yes, of course.
   I think cold food is easier.
   Hot drinks are better.
   A buffet is more convenient.
   I think fruit is healthier
4 *Your own answers.*

Unit 14

Get ready to listen and speak
○ *Your own answers.*

A

1 save money   earn a good salary   keep to a budget
2 and 3
b small c earn d salary e enough f budget g use

B

1 Paul introduces the topic with 'I'm going to talk to you about …'
No, *The next point* and *Another point* cannot be used at the beginning of the talk.
2 B, My fourth point is …
3 No, these expressions are used in more formal situations.
4 and 5 *Your own answers.*

C

1 a No b Yes c No
2 b expensive clothes, holidays, restaurants c credit card
   d month e interest f ten g year

D

1 a A. This question asks for more detail about Paul's second point – 'how much you earn'.
   b B. This question asks about a topic that Paul doesn't talk about but it is still linked to the topic of managing money.
   c A. This question asks for more detail about the last point Paul talks about – 'plan your savings'.
   d B. This question asks about a topic that Paul doesn't talk about but it is still linked to the topic of managing money.

Focus on how to ask follow-up questions

1 You talked about saving.
2 a how I can get,   b where I get
3 *Possible answers:*
   a I'd like to ask how much a good salary is.
   b I'm interested in knowing how I get a financial advisor.
   c You talked about saving. What should I invest in?
   d Do you think it's a good idea to have more than one bank account?

2 2 f 3 a 4 e 5 c 6 d
3 *Possible answers:*
   b I'm interested in knowing the best way to save for my retirement.
   c You talked about sport. How much exercise should I do each week?
   d Do you think we use mobile phones too much?
   e I'd like to ask what we can do to help clean up the environment.
   f I'd like to ask which is the easiest one to learn.
4 *Your own answers. Possible questions:*
   I'd like to ask what you do if you are not earning enough money.
   I'm interested in knowing how you should ask your employer for a pay rise.
   You talked about budgets. How do you make one?

Unit 15

Get ready to listen and speak
○ *Your own answers.*

A

1 c
2 b interview c break d Learning e social f timetables
   g canteen h conversation

B

1 You can delete <u>do</u> in A but not in B.
When the same <u>verb</u> is used for the two choices, you don't need to <u>repeat</u> it.
You can say <u>can</u> or <u>could</u> because they have a similar meaning.
<u>Option</u> has a similar meaning to <u>choice</u>.
2 In A, <u>either</u> and <u>or</u> join the two parts of the sentence.
In C, <u>and</u> joins the two parts.
3 b You could either do a conversation class in the Learning Centre or in a café.
   c You can either choose the grammar class or ask for extra help in the Learning Centre.
   d You could either borrow a dictionary from the library or buy your own from the bookshop.
   e One option is to talk to the Director of Studies about your problem and another option is to talk to your teacher.
   f You could either stay in the same class or try a higher level.
   g You can either go on the class trip or meet your friends.
   h One option is to do your homework in the Learning Centre and another option is to do it when you get home.
   i You could either play table tennis or watch the school team play football.

C

1 a speak English b on time c your mobile phone
2 That it's OK to arrive 20 minutes late.

D

1 a We aren't allowed to use our mobiles.
  b aren't allowed to
  c We have to speak English all the time.
  d have to
  e Yes, they are.
  f Toby made the rule. Bruno is repeating Toby's rule.
2 Do we have to come to every class? Are we allowed to bring some water to class?
3 *Your own answers.*

Focus on language of obligation

a *must* and *mustn't*.
b Because he is the teacher of the class and it is his rule. He has the authority to make the rule.
c Because it is not his rule. He is explaining the rule to another person.
d No. It can make you sound impolite. It is better to use *have to* and be *allowed to*.
e Do I have to be on time?
f Am I allowed to use my mobile phone?

Sound smart

1 c

---

4 b You have to arrive on time for class.
  c You're not allowed to miss more than 20% of class time.
  d You have to do some homework most nights.
  e You have to do a progress test every month.
  f You have to bring your coursebook to school every day.
  g You're not allowed to use your first language in class.
5 b Am I allowed to arrive early?
  c How often do I have to do homework?
  d Do I have to bring the coursebook every day?
  e Am I allowed to write in my coursebook?

Unit16

Get ready to listen and speak

○ *Your own answers.*
◎ *Your own answers.*

A

1 listening, speaking, vocabulary, pronunciation
2 b mistakes c translates d DVDs e five or ten
  f detail g subtitles h vocabulary

B

1 The expressions are suggestions.
  b *What some students find really useful is to* … introduces someone's opinion.
  a *I think it's important to* … introduces the speaker's opinion.

2 c Why not watch five or ten minutes of the movie?
  d The first time you listen I think it's important to listen for general information.
  e (I think) it's important not to use the subtitles the first time.
  f The second time you listen you could try to understand more detail.
  g What some students find really useful is to use the subtitles.
  h The fourth time (you listen) why not listen for new words?
3 *Possible answers:*
  What some students find really useful is to ask lots of questions.
  It's important not to worry about mistakes.
  Why not join a conversation group?
  You could talk to yourself.
  Why not record yourself speaking and then listen to it?

C

1 c, c
2 b telephone c presentations d conversation
  e did you learn? f useful was it?
  g you need to change anything?

D

1 a need to
2 dream, ambition
3 b Omar's goal is to understand lectures and presentations in English.
  c Stefan needs to speak English on the phone.
  d Li-Ying wants to write essays in English.
  e Katerina's aim is to speak English at work.
4 *Your own answers.*

Review2

Section 1

| 1 a | 3 a | 5 a | 7 c | 9 c |
| 2 c | 4 b | 6 b | 8 a | 10 b |

Section 2

11 *Your own answers. Possible answers*: I plan to study in the UK, I hope to travel a lot.
12 Could you just clear the tables faster?
13 Have you given them a menu yet?
14 Introduction, organization, giving examples.
15 Do I have to come to every lesson?
16 Why not listen to songs in English?
17 *Possible answers*: record yourself speaking, ask lots of questions
18 *Possible answers*: watch DVDs in English, listen again.

Section 3

19 a laptop
20 b
21 *Possible answer:* I'm having lunch with my friends then I'm going to an English lesson at 5 pm.
22 *Possible answer:* My dream is to study in the US or Australia.

Real skills for real life

A brand new, four-level skills series

For photocopiable skills activities, try these Copy Collection titles…

Book & Audio CD
978-0-521-60848-0

Book
978-0-521-53287-7

Book
978-0-521-53405-5

Book
978-0-521-60582-3

Book & Audio CDs (2)
978-0-521-75461-3

Book & Audio CD
978-0-521-75464-4

Book
978-0-521-55981-2
Cassette
978-0-521-55980-5

Book
978-0-521-55979-9
Cassette
978-0-521-55978-2

Book
978-0-521-62612-5
Cassettes
978-0-521-62611-8

Please order through your usual bookseller.
In case of difficulty, please contact:

**ELT Marketing, Cambridge University Press,
The Edinburgh Building,
Cambridge, CB2 8RU, UK**

**Tel: +44 (0)1223 325922
Fax: +44 (0)1223 325984**

Listening & Speaking

Level 1

With answers &
Audio CDs (2)
978-0-521-70198-3
Without answers
978-0-521-70199-0

Level 2

With answers &
Audio CDs (2)
978-0-521-70200-3
Without answers
978-0-521-70201-0

Level 3

With answers &
Audio CDs (2)
978-0-521-70588-2
Without answers
978-0-521-70589-9

Level 4

With answers &
Audio CDs (2)
978-0-521-70590-5
Without answers
978-0-521-70591-2

Writing

Level 1

With answers & Audio CD
978-0-521-70184-6
Without answers
978-0-521-70185-3

Level 2

With answers & Audio CD
978-0-521-70186-0
Without answers
978-0-521-70187-7

Level 3

With answers & Audio CD
978-0-521-70592-9
Without answers
978-0-521-70593-6

Level 4

With answers & Audio CD
978-0-521-70594-3
Without answers
978-0-521-70595-0

Reading

Level 1

With answers
978-0-521-70202-7
Without answers
978-0-521-70203-4

Level 2

With answers
978-0-521-70204-1
Without answers
978-0-521-70205-8

Level 3

With answers
978-0-521-70573-8
Without answers
978-0-521-70574-5

Level 4

With answers
978-0-521-70575-2
Without answers
978-0-521-70576-9

Bring your skills to life

For teacher's notes, visit: **www.cambridge.org/englishskills**